Automotive Wiring
A Practical Guide to Wiring Your Hot Rod or Custom Car

By Dennis W. Parks

Dedication

To Dad, the hardest-working man I ever knew.

Quarto.com

© 2011 Quarto Publishing Group USA Inc.
Text and illustrations © 2011 Dennis W. Parks

First published in 2011 by Motorbooks, an imprint of
The Quarto Group, 100 Cummings Center, Suite 265-D,
Beverly, MA 01915, USA. T (978) 282-9590 F (978) 283-
2742

Motorbooks titles are also available at discount for retail,
wholesale, promotional, and bulk purchase. For details,
contact the Special Sales Manager by email at specialsales@
quarto.com or by mail at The Quarto Group, Attn: Special
Sales Manager, 100 Cummings Center, Suite 265-D,
Beverly, MA 01915, USA.

ISBN-13: 978-0-7603-3992-3

Editor: Steve Casper and Chris Endres
Design Manager: Brad Springer
Layout: Gracia L.A. Lindberg
Front cover photo: Randy Johnson
Photos on page 5 and 6: Shutterstock images
Photo on page 89: Brad Remy/shutterstock.com

Contents

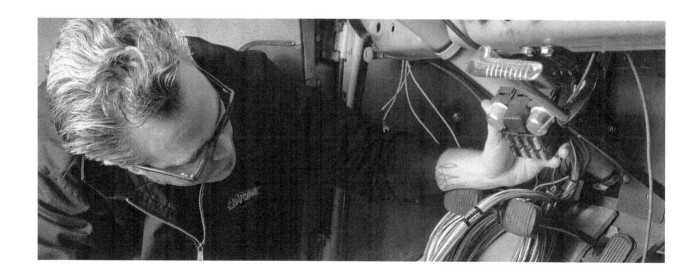

Foreword

You have in your hand a great resource. I did not have what you now hold when I did my first complete wiring job. I still drive the vehicle on which I did that first complete wiring harness more than 20 years ago. It was crude by today's standards, but it was safe and has not failed me. I often look at some of my work and think how I would do it differently now. On that first job I used a modified factory fusebox and a factory schematic as a guide. I did not have the Internet to use, nor did I have a book as a resource to help me. This book would have made that job so much easier. I learned a lot then, but I could have learned it easier and faster with this book as a guide.

Wiring is not a tough physical job, but it does require some mental exercise. You must plan ahead and prepare each part so that it does not become a problem later. I like to approach the job with the attitude that when it is finished, the wiring should not call attention to itself. It is there, but it does not draw your eye to it when you look at the vehicle. In addition, the wiring that is visible should be neat and done well.

Along with the information in this book, I have some advice: Take your time and check everything you do. Plan ahead and think through the routing of the wiring and how each circuit will work. Check each connector after you crimp it. Give each one a light tug to make sure it is crimped tightly and that the wires do not move in the crimp. When the job is done, before I attach the last cable to the battery, I check with a test light and a meter for current draw with everything turned off. Then I attach a test lead with an inline fuse between the battery and the cable. I purposely use a small fuse in this circuit. If something is wrong, I want to know it right away. It is just a small safeguard in case there is something wired incorrectly. Not only are you checking your wiring job, but you are also checking all the components in the electrical system.

There is a lot of satisfaction in doing a complete wiring job yourself. It is not rocket science or something to be afraid of, but rather a job that is rewarding when it is completed. You can do it and this book will help you. The greatest reward will come after you have some experience and others turn to you for help and advice.

—*John Kimbrough, 2011*
Veteran hot rodder, retired shop teacher, and automotive book fact checker

Acknowledgments

While doing research for this (and other) books, I have found that many authors really make the subject more difficult than it needs to be. Sure, a little bit of theory and the obligatory safety precautions are necessary, but there is a vast difference between the guy who needs to rewire a portion of his daily driver and the guy who wants to design electrical systems for a vehicle manufacturer. Since I can more closely relate to the guy in the driveway or garage adding some electrical accessory than I can to an electrical engineer, the former is whom this book is written for. If you want to be an engineer, go to school and read the textbooks. If you want to know how to rewire your own vehicle, read this book.

I have the good fortune of knowing a vast group of guys who have been tinkering with automobiles in one form or another for longer than any of us care to admit. Luckily for me, they will usually answer my questions, no matter how many times I ask. In no particular order, a great big thank-you goes out to Rich Fox at Affordable Street Rods, Chris Shelton, Ed Thornton, Bob Galbraith at New Port Engineering, Keith Moritz at Morfab Customs, John and Sam Kimbrough, and Jack and Donnie Karg at Karg's Hot Rod Shop. All of these guys contributed to this book in one way or another. For some, it was during time spent walking around countless rod runs, others while I was photographing work being done in their shop, and still others during numerous phone calls, e-mails, and shop visits. Again, thank you for sharing your collective wealth of information. Finally, thank you to John Kimbrough, Jim Exler, Todd Hildebrandt, Satch Reed, and Rex Vint for reading through the manuscript to make sure everything made sense before I submitted it to the publisher.

—*Dennis W. Parks, 2011*

Introduction

Saying that automotive wiring is something that mystifies many people is an understatement if there ever was one. Yet, it really doesn't need to be so mysterious. Wiring and electricity are simple subjects and can be done by most anyone willing to take the necessary time. The tools required are not exotic or expensive, so not having a roll-around chest full of tools is no excuse for not knowing your way around a wiring opportunity.

Wiring (automotive or otherwise) must be done in a methodical manner to avoid problems. So, if you are an impatient person or want to see results immediately, doing it yourself may not be for you. If you can safely modify your vehicle's electrical system, however, there is virtually no limit to the electrical gadgets available to you and your passengers.

In Chapter 1, we'll discuss the basics so that you get off on the right foot. This will include a bit of electrical theory, an overview of components, and then tools and equipment. Chapter 2 will discuss the major components of typical ignition and charging systems and how those components interact with each other. Likewise, Chapters 3 and 4 will discuss lighting circuits and switches, respectively.

The information included in these chapters will not only assist you in traditional applications, it will be useful in designing custom applications as well. Chapter 5 will discuss engine monitoring systems, while Chapter 6 will discuss specific, yet common accessory circuits. Chapter 7 discusses audio and video installations. Chapter 8 discusses some specific types of wiring, ranging from using a vehicle-specific kit to completely rewiring a vehicle, to using a universal kit, to do-it-yourself, and then the book wraps up with some troubleshooting tips.

Whether you simply need to make some minor repairs to your daily driver, are restoring the vehicle of your dreams, or are building a vehicle from scratch, this book has plenty of electrical wiring information for you. I hope you enjoy the book, and thank you for buying it.

Chapter 1
Automotive Electric Basics

While many automobile enthusiasts will insist that they do all of the mechanical work, bodywork, or perhaps even upholstery work on their automobiles, they will quickly admit that they do not do any electrical work. To a certain extent, that is understandable, as wiring is generally thought of as boring and is certainly not as flashy as having a multicolored paint job atop flawless bodywork. However, the slickest paint job or the most comfy tuck-and-roll interior won't get you home when your vehicle blows a fuse 50 miles from nowhere. Even if you have no intention of wiring your late-model daily driver or vintage hot rod, being familiar with your vehicle's electrical system and having an idea of how it is supposed to work may save you a tow charge sometime.

AUTOMOBILE ELECTRICITY PRINCIPLES

Whenever it comes to writing a book about wiring, the author is pretty much obligated to mention Ohm's Law and Kirchhoff's Law. That being said, I'll attempt to get the textbook stuff out of the way in the next few paragraphs. They are laws and they do describe how electricity works, so there is no need for me to re-create the wheel.

Ohm's Law describes the relationship of voltage, current, and resistance. Voltage (typically expressed as E in equations) is the difference in potential and is not surprisingly measured in volts. Current (typically expressed as I in equations) is the flow of electrons and is measured in amperes (or amps). Resistance (typically expressed as R in equations) is the opposition to the flow of electrons and is measured in ohms. Ohm's Law states that current is equal to voltage divided by resistance. As long as you know the values for any two of these components, you can determine the third. The original formula and its derivations are as follows:

I = E / R or Current = Voltage / Resistance
E = I x R or Voltage = Current x Resistance
R = E / I or Resistance = Voltage / Current

Kirchhoff's Law is somewhat more complicated and for the purposes of automotive wiring (and this book) we'll discuss Kirchhoff's Voltage Law and Kirchhoff's Current Law. The first states that the sum of voltages applied to a circuit equals the sum of the voltage dropped across the components within that circuit. The second states that current entering a junction in a circuit equals the current leaving a junction.

It would seem readily apparent that Ohm's Law is important when designing an electrical system to ensure that enough voltage is able to pass through the necessary length of wire without causing a fire. While you may not readily see the importance of Kirchhoff's Law, rest assured that it will prove handy when troubleshooting an electrical problem. Of course, Ohm's Law will be important then as well.

Wire Size

Wire used in an automobile is often called primary wire. The wire size is referred to as gauge (or gage) and is typically between 2- and 22-gauge. Just as with sheet-metal products, the smaller the number, the larger the wire. A large no. 2 wire would be used to connect the vehicle's battery to the starter or as a ground wire for the battery, while 22-gauge wire would be common to wire the lights of the instrument panel in the dash.

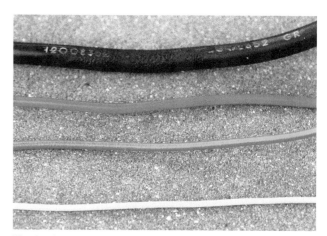

Wire sizes from 2-gauge (large) to 22-gauge (small) are common in automotive wiring. These sample wires show just four sizes. The black wire at the top is a no. 2 or 4-gauge and would typically be used to connect the battery to the starter or to ground. The red wire is 10-gauge, commonly used in the ignition circuit. The blue wire is 12-gauge, while the yellow wire is 16-gauge.

CIRCUIT PROTECTION

As current passes through a wire, the current generates heat. If this current is beyond the acceptable limits of that particular wire, the heat generated could potentially start a fire. To prevent this, various types of components can be installed within an electrical circuit. These components are fuses, fusible links, diodes, and circuit breakers. Each is designed for different situations and should be used accordingly.

Fuses and Fusible Links

These two circuit-protection components are the most similar and, by design, serve as the weak link in the electrical circuit. They are designed to allow only a predetermined amount of current to flow through the circuit. Within the fuse panel, wiring is connected so that one side of the fuse connects directly to the accessory or load side. The opposite side of the fuse connects to power. Between the two contacts of a fuse is a conductive strip of metal that will melt at a prescribed temperature. If and when too much current passes through the fuse, resistance through this metal strip will cause enough heat to melt the metal strip, causing the fuse to "blow" before the entire circuit heats up. In essence, the fuse is designed to fail in order to protect the rest of that particular circuit. Since you could envision this metal strip

as a bridge between power and load, it should make sense that when the metal strip melts in two, the circuit is broken and the flow of electricity stops in that particular circuit.

As you would imagine, fuses are available for different amp ratings, such as 5, 10, 15, 20, and so on, regardless of construction type. While there are some technical differences in the physical and compositional makeup of the metal strips within the fuse, we'll just say that a fuse with a smaller rating typically has a thinner metal strip or wire, while a fuse with a higher rating typically has a thicker or wider metal strip. This is true in both the older glass tube–type fuses and the newer blade fuses. The amperage rating of a fuse is marked on the outside of the fuse, however, so you do not need to measure the metal strip for any reason.

Current (in Amps)	Length of Wire (in Feet)					
	up to 4	4–7	7–10	10–13	13–16	16–19
0–20	14 ga.	12 ga.	12 ga.	10 ga.	10 ga.	8 ga.
20–35	12 ga.	10 ga.	8 ga.	8 ga.	6 ga.	6 ga.
35–50	10 ga.	8 ga.	8 ga.	6 ga.	6 ga.	4 ga.
50–65	8 ga.	8 ga.	6 ga.	4 ga.	4 ga.	4 ga.
65–85	6 ga.	6 ga.	4 ga.	4 ga.	2 ga.	2 ga.
85–105	6 ga.	6 ga.	4 ga.	2 ga.	2 ga.	2 ga.
105–125	4 ga.	4 ga.	4 ga.	2 ga.	2 ga.	2 ga.
125–150	2 ga.	2 ga.	2 ga.	2 ga.	0 ga.	0 ga.

AWL	Resistance (Per Foot)
20	0.010360 ohms
18	0.006520 ohms
16	0.004080 ohms
14	0.002580 ohms
12	0.001620 ohms
10	0.001020 ohms
8	0.000640 ohms
6	0.000402 ohms
4	0.000253 ohms
2	0.000159 ohms
1	0.000126 ohms
0	0.000100 ohms

To determine the correct wire size for your application, you should first determine the maximum current flow (amperage) through the cable. Then determine the length of the cable that routing through your vehicle will require and consult the chart to determine the minimum required wire size. You should always use a larger wire (numerically smaller) if the minimum recommended wire is not available.

This table shows the amount of resistance caused by each foot of wire for any particular wire gauge. While these may seem like small numbers per foot, they can prove useful when troubleshooting a fuel pump, electric fan, or other electric device that simply is not getting adequate power.

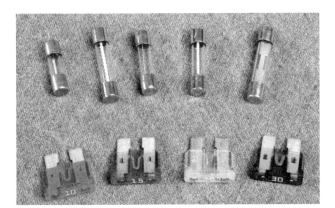

While somewhat difficult to distinguish in the photo of these glass fuses, the conductive metal strip is easier to recognize in the plastic blade–type fuses. This metal strip is typically smaller and/or thinner in smaller-capacity fuses and larger/thicker in larger-capacity fuses.

The amperage (amp) rating for fuses is typically stamped right into the fuse's color-coded housing.

On glass tube fuses, the amp rating is stamped into the metal end cap, which can be difficult to read, especially if it has been subjected to moisture and is developing rust.

Vehicles manufactured prior to 1980 typically used glass fuses that were small (approximately 1/4 inch diameter), in various lengths, and in various amp ratings. Multiple types of glass fuses are available, with AGC being the most common. These glass fuses include a metal cap on each end that makes electrical contact with the fuse panel. While these fuses worked as designed, a common problem was the formation of rust on the metal cap, which could cause problems that could be difficult to diagnose. Glass fuses gave way to ATC-, ATM-, and ATO-blade fuses. These fuses are made of a type of plastic, so they are more durable than glass fuses. In addition to their amperage ratings, blade-type fuses can be different physical sizes depending on which type of fuse panel they are to be used with. Fuses and their respective fuse panels are referred to as ATC, Mini ATC, and MAXI, with MAXIs being the largest. Since these are plug-in components, they are not interchangeable between sizes. Electrically, they work the same way.

Later-model vehicles utilize fuses of various sizes, as well as different amp ratings. Shown are ATM Mini, standard ATC/ATO, and Maxi fuses. Due to the various sizes, when in doubt take the blown-out fuses with you when you go to purchase a replacement.

Fusible links are available in auto parts stores as a short piece of wire with a terminal crimped on for use when connecting to the starter, or simply as a roll of wire so that you can crimp on your own connector.

A fusible link works in the same way as a fuse but is designed to be placed inline rather than in a fuse panel. Instead of a metal strip between contacts, the fusible link is made of wire that is four wire sizes smaller than what the circuit calls for and is surrounded by nonflammable insulation. When excessive current passes through the fusible link, the inner wire will melt, stopping the flow of electricity. A fusible link is typically used in a situation that calls for a heavier load and therefore larger wire (8- or 10-gauge), such as power to the starter solenoid from the ignition switch.

While any situation that causes a fuse to blow, break, or burn out should be remedied before moving on, fuses and fusible links present different situations. You should always attempt to determine what caused the fuse to blow and then fix that situation, but you may not be able to address it right now.

Many circuits protected by fuses in contemporary automobiles are for creature comforts. So, if the power seat adjustment circuit shorts out and blows a fuse, it is not a big deal if you cannot trace the wires until the weekend. On the other hand, let's say you are making some modifications to your ride and you inadvertently scrape some insulation from an ignition wire or a wire to the headlights. Of course you don't realize that you did it until it grounds out and a fuse blows.

You find the bare spot on the wire and realize that a couple of passes with electrical tape will alleviate the problem. You are a genius, but you don't have another fuse and it is 20 miles to the nearest auto parts store. Then you realize that fuses are interchangeable and the one you just blew is the same amp rating as the power seat adjustment circuit. You have not adjusted the seat since you bought the car, so you are in luck. Simply pull the fuse from a non-critical circuit, insert it where it needs to be, and you are back on the road. Just make sure that the fuses are indeed the same amp rating. If you use a fuse that is too small, it will blow out, while using a fuse that is too big will leave you unprotected.

Fusible links, like fuses, are interchangeable, but since they are installed inline they must be replaced when one goes bad. It is rare that a fusible link will blow out, but when it does you will need to alleviate the problem before proceeding.

Diodes

A diode serves as a one-way valve to allow electrical current to flow one way only. Like fuses, they are sized based on voltage ratings. Since current can flow only one way through a diode, it must be installed in the correct orientation. Current flows from the anode end toward the cathode end, which is designated by a white stripe. As current passes through light emitting diodes (LEDs), they emit light. See more about this in Chapter 3.

Diodes can be used to isolate current or prevent voltage spikes. Motor homes and stretch limousines commonly have multiple batteries to provide power for the many electrical accessories. Each battery can be charged by one lone alternator by using a diode for each battery. Connect each battery to the cathode end of a diode and connect the anode end of each diode to the alternator. In circuits where electromagnetic switches are used, residual current that is present whenever power is shut off (such as turning off the ignition) could cause a power surge or voltage spike. By installing a diode, damage to the circuit can be prevented. See more about this in Chapter 4.

Circuit Breakers

You could think of circuit breakers as momentary fuses. While fuses essentially break their contacts as they do their job to protect a circuit, a circuit breaker simply opens the contacts to stop current flow temporarily. The contacts are connected by a metal strip, much like a fuse. The difference is that when current exceeds the capacity of the circuit breaker, the metal strip changes shape and momentarily breaks the electrical connection. When the metal strip cools sufficiently, it changes back to its original shape, thereby resetting or restoring the electrical connection.

Two types of circuit breakers are available: auto resetting and manual resetting. Auto resetting circuit breakers are commonly used by original equipment manufacturers (OEMs) to protect circuits with high-current demand. This would include headlights, power windows, and power seats. Manual-reset circuit breakers must be pushed back into position manually when they are tripped. This type can be found in systems that shut off fuel pumps when the vehicle is in impacted or other security systems.

This is the stock circuit breaker for the horn in the '68 Chevy truck that is being rewired as part of this book project. The red wire goes to the fuse panel and the green goes to the horn.

CIRCUIT CONTROL

Many of the electrical circuits in our vehicles require a surge of current initially for just a short amount of time, while others require a constant amount of current the entire time they are operating. When a large amount of current is required, albeit for a short time, it is not desirable to send all of that current through the entire circuit. Relays and solenoids are two methods of controlling the amount of current flowing through a specific circuit.

Relays

Relays are a type of switch that can be used to pass large amounts of current to a specific accessory, without overloading a conventional switch or wiring harness. Typical relays have two circuits: one that carries the large amount of current from the battery to accessory (such as a fuel pump or fan) and a second circuit that switches the flow of current. When the relay is switched on, electrical current from the power source (battery) passes through the relay to operate a

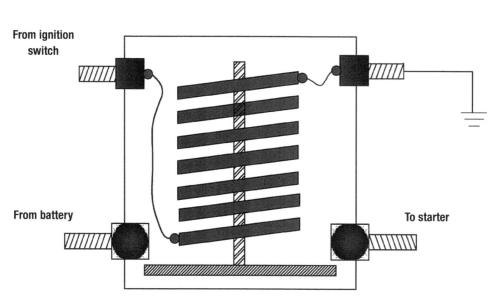

From ignition switch

From battery

To starter

A Ford-style ignition solenoid includes a coil of wire that receives power from the ignition switch and is also connected to a ground source. When the key is switched off, there is no electrical connection between the battery and the starter.

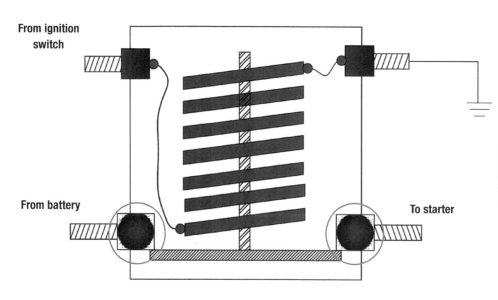

From ignition switch

From battery

To starter

When the ignition key is turned to start the engine, the coil of wire generates a magnetic field to pull the disc upward, closing the circuit between the battery and the starter.

switch within the relay. Electric current then flows directly to the accessory, without passing through the entire wiring harness. See more about relays in Chapter 4.

Solenoids

Solenoids are specialized switches that can be used to physically move an object by means of an electromagnetic field. All conventional automobiles use this type of switch to turn on the starter. Custom cars of days gone by and many contemporary vehicles use this type of switch in power door latches and trunk latches. The noticeable click that you hear when you press the remote control of your power door locks is the solenoid in action.

Any solenoid switch includes a coil that when energized creates a magnetic field. Within this coil is a plunger with a copper disc on one end. When power is applied to the solenoid, the magnetic field pulls the plunger into the coil. The copper disc then bridges the gap between the two terminals: one load and one power, thus turning the starter or locking and unlocking the doors. See more about solenoids in Chapter 4.

COMPONENTS

Now that we have at least touched on some of the basics that would be required to design an automotive wiring system, we should discuss the physical parts that are used in that wiring system. At the very basic wiring installation or repair is wire, fuse panel, and connectors.

Wire

Unlike today's computers and other audio-visual tools and toys that can be operated wirelessly, an automobile's electrical needs are met by passing electrical current through wire, and lots of it. Sure, some vehicles will require more circuits than others, but it all passes through multi-strand copper wire.

While the uninitiated may believe that wire is wire and it doesn't matter what kind you use, that is simply not correct. You should know the difference between GPT (general purpose thermoplastic) and XL (cross-linked polyethylene) series wire. GPT wire should be avoided, as its insulation is thermoplastic. What this means is that it gets brittle as it oxidizes and its melting point is very low. As if that weren't enough, GPT wire is stiff and therefore more difficult to work with.

Wire that is much better is the XL series, which has a cross-linked (thermoset) polyolefin insulation. Within this XL series are three different thicknesses of wire: SXL (standard wall), GXL (thin wall), and TXL (extra thin wall). As an example of the wall thickness, 16-gauge SXL has a nominal OD of 0.119 inch. GXL and TXL 16-gauge wires would have nominal OD 0.103 inch and 0.088 inch respectively. This type of insulation allows the wire to stay soft and flexible throughout its life. Additionally, XL wire has a much higher melting point, making it significantly better suited for under-hood applications, where engine temperature could wreak havoc with lesser wire.

A relay is used to control large amounts of current without overloading a switch or wiring harness that would otherwise be overloaded. Relays are especially useful when wiring headlights, fuel pumps, fans, or any other accessories that have high current requirements.

Electrical current passes along the surface of the wire, so multi-strand wire is able to pass much more current than single-strand copper wire, such as that used in residential wiring.

Regardless of the gauge of the wire, primary wire is comprised of several much smaller strands of copper wire within its insulation. Many finer strands provide more surface area than larger thicker strands, and since electricity flows along the surface of the copper strands, this is a good thing. Combining the thinner wire strands with the thinner insulation material allows an overall thinner wire to carry as much current as the older, thicker wire. This will also allow you to run the same amount of wires in a smaller bundle that takes up less room in crowded locations and will lie flatter under carpet or upholstery. Who wants the interior of their vehicle to look like there are snakes under the carpet?

Automotive wire is available in several different colors, several different gauges—as mentioned previously, and in different lengths. Each automobile manufacturer will have its color codes for specific circuits. Likewise, someone who does custom wiring may have his or her own color codes that may be the same as or different from anyone elses. The electric current doesn't know (or care) what color wire it is passing through, so the color of wire does not really matter.

Systematically using different colors will make troubleshooting and repair much easier, however, whether your vehicle is up on jack stands in your garage or sitting on the shoulder of a busy freeway. Believe it or not, I have heard stories of custom vehicles that were wired exclusively with one color wire. As if that were not bad enough, it was usually the same color as the paint on the vehicle.

Most any auto parts store will have at least a few rolls of primary wire in stock, but will usually be about 30 feet long at the most, with many rolls being much shorter. Unless you are in the business of wiring automobiles, these short rolls will typically meet your needs. If you do wiring on a regular basis, spools of wire are much more economical when purchased through a wiring supply house. This will prove to be true for most all electrical components, such as connectors, switches, and fuses.

Fuse Panel

The fuse panel serves as the distribution center for all things electrical in your automobile. Whether you are dealing with a late-model vehicle, a race car, or a hot rod, it will require some sort of fuse panel. Unless you make your own, each terminal on the fuse panel will be labeled so that it is easy to determine one circuit from another.

This is the fuse panel from my "in the process of being rewired" '68 Chevy pickup. A mere nine fuses protected the electrical system of that vintage truck, while my '08 Silverado has considerably more fuses and circuit breakers. The essential wiring is preterminated into the fuse panel, while spade terminals allow for connection of more circuits.

This is a universal fuse panel mounted on the interior side of the firewall on a fiberglass-bodied Track T roadster. The fuse block is mounted near the center of an aluminum panel and is then electrically connected to two terminal strips. Each connection on the terminal strip can be made by loosening a screw and then sliding the appropriate wire with fork connector under the screw and then tightening it.

Aftermarket fuse panels may or may not have the electrical wire preterminated at the fuse panel. In this case, preterminated means that the wires are already connected at the fuse panel. Some wiring kits will have only the internal wiring of the fuse panel connected, but none of the wires that run out through the vehicle are connected. This depends significantly on whether the kit is vehicle-specific or is of universal design. Each type has its pros and cons, so if you are rewiring a vehicle, do some shopping around to see what is available before you buy.

If the wires are preterminated or pre-installed, you would simply mount the fuse panel, route the wires to the specific accessories, cut to length, install the appropriate connector, and then connect to the accessory. If the wires are not preterminated or pre-installed, the process would be the same, but only after connecting the wire to the appropriate terminal on the fuse panel first. See more about wiring installations in Chapter 8.

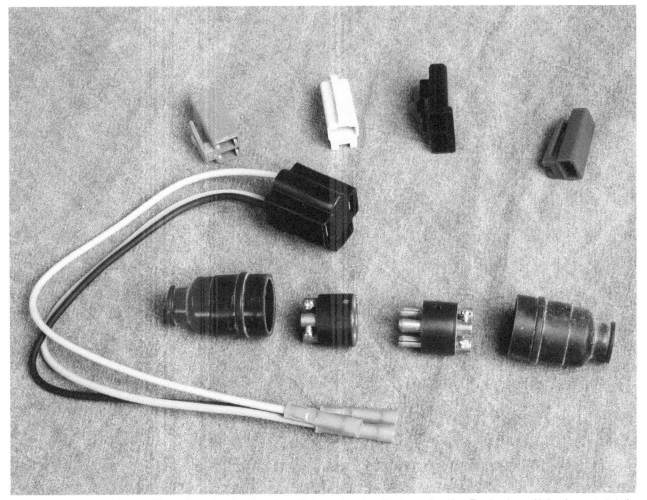

Multi-wire plugs are available in many different sizes and configurations. Across the top are four plugs of various configurations. The plug shown with the wires connects to the back of a conventional headlight, with the wires connecting to high beam, low beam, or ground. The four-piece plug could be used as a quick disconnect for up to four wires.

Connectors

Connectors are the means by which wire attaches to the power source on one end and the load on the other end. In various types of wiring, soldering is more common, but for now I am talking about crimp-on connectors. Soldering will be discussed later in Chapter 8, as contrary to some beliefs, soldering does have its place in automotive wiring.

Any auto parts store that carries automotive wiring will also carry at least a minimum assortment of connectors that are intended to be crimped onto the end of a stripped wire. These will include butt connectors, ring connectors, fork connectors, push-on terminals (both male and female), and bullet connectors (both male and female). These are all intended to be used with one wire, although the next size larger connector can be used if two wires are to be connected to the same terminal. Some terminals, such as spade terminals, will allow for only one connector, while others such as studs can allow for multiple connectors. Better crimp-on connectors have serrations on the inside of the crimping barrel to help prevent the wire from slipping out, while the cheaper connectors are smooth on the inside. After crimping any type of connector onto a wire, you should give it a slight tug to ensure that the connector is crimped sufficiently. If it comes off now, it can easily be replaced and crimped correctly. However, if you do not test it now and it is loose, it will undoubtedly fail, and probably at the most inopportune time or location.

Crimp-on or solderless connectors are color-coded so they can be easily associated with the applicable wire sizes. Red connectors are to be used with small wire between 22- and 18-gauge. Blue connectors are to be used with wire between 16- and 12-gauge, while yellow connectors are to be used with wire between 10- and 6-gauge. Larger wires (such as battery cables) may also use larger red connectors, but commonly use connections that are soldered in place.

Plugs are designed for situations that call for multiple wires of the same circuit to be disconnected easily. An example of this is at the steering column where turn signals, headlights, horn, and so on would need to be disconnected if the steering column was removed. Another would be the common occurrence of trailer wiring, where taillights, stoplights, and electric brakes use individual wires but would be connected or disconnected as a whole. Plugs can be a matched set of male and female or simply a more universal design of multiple female connections that would fit onto the spade connections of a circuit breaker, ignition switch, or other accessory that requires multiple wires.

Butt Connectors: Butt connectors are used to permanently join two pieces of wire inline, such as when connecting to a headlight plug that typically already has a short piece of wire preterminated into each of the three terminals. Another use for butt connectors would be when one piece of wire simply is not long enough and you need to add a piece of wire to it.

Ring Connectors: Ring connectors are used most commonly in circuits that you do not want to become disconnected easily. Regardless of size, the ring is held in place on the terminal by a screw or bolt, so it is necessary to remove that fastener to disconnect the circuit. A common use is for the power wire that connects to the back of the alternator.

Fork Connectors: Fork connectors are much like a ring connector, but with a portion of the ring missing. They are held in place by a screw or bolt that must be loosened (but not removed) to disconnect the circuit. These are commonly used on terminal strips or fuse panels that are of universal design.

Push-on Terminals: Push-on terminals are probably the most common type of connector used in automotive wiring. After being crimped onto a wire, they require no tools to connect or disconnect. They are simply, as the name implies, push-on (or pull-off). By design, they allow for a secure connection, yet can be easily disconnected when necessary. These are commonly found in fuse panels and other components such as stop light switches, horns, and circuit breakers. Note that most male/female type connectors are situated so that no male connector is used on a wire that could be energized while that same male connector is disconnected.

Bullet Connectors: Bullet connections require a matched set of male/female connectors. They work in similar fashion to a butt connector, but allow for quick disconnect. This would make them suitable for most any circuit that may need to be removed from the vehicle for service, such as a dash panel and its gauges or headlights from a street-legal hot rod that may be raced at the drag strip or on a dry lake on occasion.

Butt connectors are used to join wires inline or can be used as a "Y" connection, such as headlight power that is split into the driver's side and passenger's side. Butt connectors require crimping on each end to secure both wires in place.

These ring connectors are designed for use as battery cable connectors. They are designed to slip over a 2- or 4-gauge wire and be soldered in place. Other similar connectors can be crimped on, but require a different type of crimper than that required for smaller (10–22-gauge) wire.

Ring connectors must be chosen for the correct wire size (red, blue, or yellow) and then for the size stud that they are to be connected to. The two blue connectors at the bottom of the photo are designed to be used with 12- to 16-gauge wire, but for distinctly different size studs. The yellow connector just above them is designed for 6- to 10-gauge wire, but for a stud somewhere between the two blue ones.

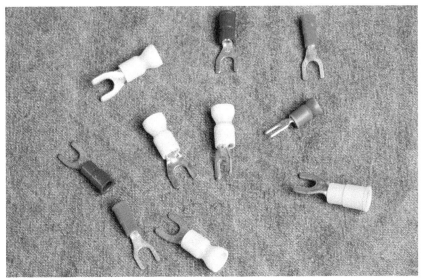

Much like ring connectors, fork connectors must be chosen for wire size and also for the width between the forks. This type of connector is typically used on fuse panels or terminal strips where it may be useful to remove a specific wire from the connection. Simply loosen a screw and pull the wire away from its connection.

For automotive wiring, push-on connectors are probably the most commonly used. Like other connectors, they are selected based on wire size, but they provide a connection that can easily be connected or disconnected.

Male push-on connectors have one metal prong that would fit within one of the female connectors. Like all other crimp-on connectors, compatible wire size is indicated by red, blue, or yellow insulation.

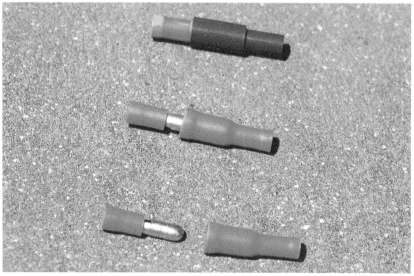

Shown are three pairs of bullet connectors, with the male of each pair on the left and the female counterpart on the right. Each would have a stripped wire inserted into the connector and then be crimped on to secure the wire. Bullet connectors are commonly used as a quick disconnect in situations where it may be necessary to remove an electrical device for service.

WIRE PROTECTION

Whether we are talking about the wiring in your daily driver or a show car that is seldom driven, the wires still need to be protected. One of the most common sources of electrical-related problems in an automobile is the wire's insulation being scraped off and exposing the bare wire. Besides the fact that a bare spot can be very difficult to find, in most cases it can be prevented.

Heat Shrink Tubing

This is one of the quick ways to distinguish a professional wiring job from one done by a hack—the presence of heat shrink tubing. This is available in different colors, different diameters, and in different lengths. I purchase it in bulk and in black, as I have no multiple specs of color throughout the vehicle. Regardless of the color, heat shrink tubing helps protect the union between wire and connector and also provides a bit of strain relief.

To use heat shrink tubing properly, cut a piece of the appropriate diameter tubing so that it is about one and a half times as long as the insulated portion of the connector. Slide this over the wire, strip the wire approximately a quarter inch, crimp on the connector, then slip the tubing over the connector and apply heat to shrink the tubing.

Miles of heat shrink tubing have no doubt been shrunk by cigarettes, cigarette lighters, and hair dryers. However, by spending $30 or less at your local auto parts store to purchase a heat gun, you can do it properly, more efficiently, and usually without burning yourself.

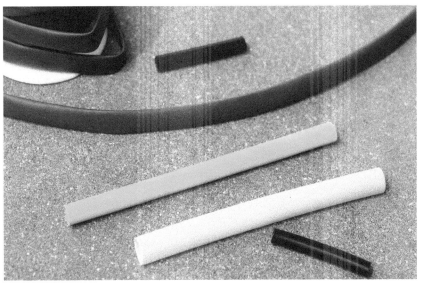

Like crimp-on connectors, heat shrink tubing is available in red, blue, and yellow sizes to coordinate with the connectors it would be used to protect. However, it is also available in black in short pieces or in bulk. If you are going to be using much of this, it will ultimately be less expensive to purchase in bulk rolls.

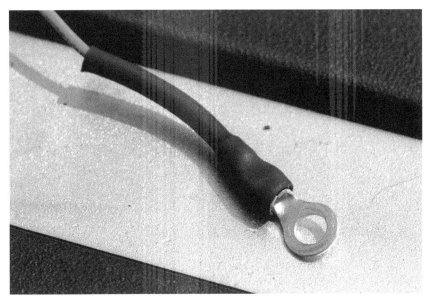

Doesn't heat shrink tubing look a lot better than some electrical tape around a terminal connection? Slide heat-shrink tubing over the end of the wire, bare the wire the correct amount, crimp the appropriate connector in place, then slide the heat shrink into the correct position, and heat. Very easy, very efficient.

Wire Wrap

Wire wrap, split loom, or convoluted tubing is the plastic tubing that is split so that it can be slid over the wiring loom after installation. In addition to looking better in appearance than a bundle of multi-colored wires, wire wrap does help to protect wires from grease, grime, and abrasions that could quickly render your vehicle or one of its accessories dead in the water.

Grommets

Anytime—and I do mean anytime, without exception—that wires pass through sheet metal or fiberglass, the wires should pass through a rubber grommet as well. If left unprotected, a wire passing through sheet metal will quickly vibrate enough to abrade the wire's insulation and short out. Even though the wire would not ground itself to a fiberglass component, it could still abrade the insulation, making itself vulnerable to moisture.

Grommets are available in different sizes and for different thicknesses of sheet metal or fiberglass. Choose a grommet that has a hole that is big enough for the wire or wires that will pass through it and has a groove wide enough to fit over the sheet metal. Then drill a hole in the sheet metal that is between the size of the wall of the grommet and its outside diameter.

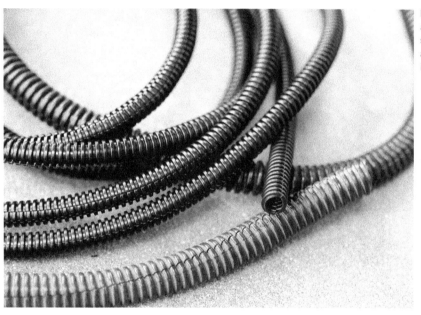

Plastic split loom provides an inexpensive method to cover and protect wires from grease, oil, and rubbing directly on something that could cause the wire to short out. The split allows the protective wrap to be installed after the wire is in place.

It cannot be overemphasized that grommets should be used anytime wires pass through sheet metal to prevent the edge of the sheet metal from rubbing through the wire's insulation and causing an electrical short. Grommets must be chosen for the correct opening diameter to allow the wire to pass through it and must also be long enough in section for the inner tube portion to pass entirely through the sheet metal.

TOOLS AND TEST EQUIPMENT

One of the great things about wiring a vehicle is that it doesn't require a bunch of expensive tools. As the basics, you need a method of cutting wire, a method of stripping wire, and a method of crimping on a connector. In a pinch or to make an emergency repair, a pair of universal wire crimpers that can be purchased for less than $10 will work. As you begin to do more electrical work, you will eventually need screwdrivers and wrenches appropriate for the vehicle you are working on. If you get serious about wiring, you may choose to add a test light, test meter, battery charger, and other specialized equipment to your collection of available tools. Regardless of what kind of work you are doing, learn to work smarter, not harder.

Wire Cutters

There are a variety of tools that cut wire. Some cut and strip, while some cut, strip, and crimp. My current favorite is simply a pair of Craftsman diagonal side cutters.

Wire Strippers

While I have quit using my universal wiring pliers for multiple tasks, I still use them for stripping wire. The main reason is that the wire size is indicated on that part of the tool and it still works great when stripping wire. If and when they wear out or quit stripping wire efficiently, I'll replace them with a pair of dedicated wire strippers.

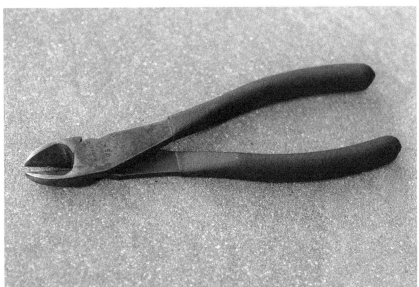

These handy diagonal side cutters work great for cutting electrical wire. As long as you do not try cutting nails, they will perform adequately for a long time.

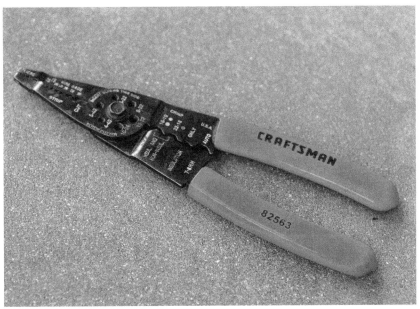

For occasional wiring needs, a pair of universal wiring pliers will most likely serve your needs and are available almost anywhere that wire is sold and for a low price. They can cut wire, strip wire, and crimp on connectors.

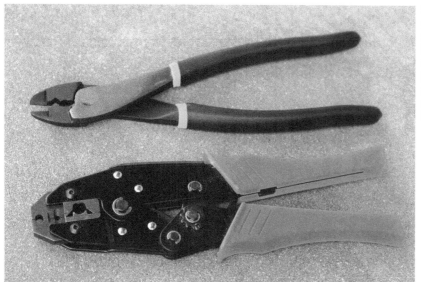

Shown are two of my personal favorite wiring tools: a pair of wire crimpers along with a ratcheting spark plug wire crimper. The design of the Greenlee pliers (top) allows the user to crimp connectors onto the wire without over-crimping them. The ratcheting spark plug wire crimpers do the same thing, but also verify that you do crimp the connector adequately, or it will not release. The latter tool can also be used with crimp-on connectors by changing the crimping head.

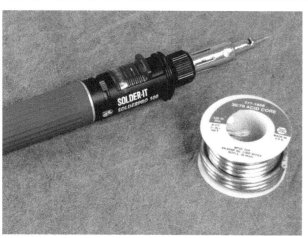

Shown are a soldering iron and solder. For electrical applications, use 60/40 lead-based, rosin-core solder. The 30/70 acid core shown is more appropriate for plumbing repairs.

Electrical tape is typically used to insulate a connection after being soldered or having solderless connectors crimped on. Heat shrink tubing is a better option, but electrical tape still works and can be more easily found if you break down while away from home.

Wire Crimpers

By the time you wire a complete vehicle, you will probably decide that there must be a better crimper than the aforementioned universal wiring tool. With some crimpers, it is all too easy to squeeze the pliers too tight or not tight enough. In either situation, you have not made a high-quality and long-lasting connection. Although they are a little more expensive, a pair of ratcheting wire crimpers will help to ensure properly crimped connections.

Soldering Iron and Related Items

With the advent of solderless connections (also called crimp-on connections), soldering of electrical connections is not as common as it once was. If done properly and with the correct solder, however, a soldered connection will last indefinitely.

Heat Gun

If you are going to use heat shrink tubing in your wiring projects, a heat gun is virtually a necessity to get the tubing to shrink properly. Your wife or girlfriend's hair dryer won't get hot enough and matches simply are not practical.

Electrical Tape

Personally, I try to avoid using any electrical tape during an automotive wiring project. Simply put, if a crimp-on connector is crimped on correctly, there is no need to wrap it with electrical tape. Electrical tape does have a time and a place where its use is justified, however. I would classify those times as being in a pinch. If you need to make a temporary, side-of-the-road repair, a roll of electrical tape may be what keeps you from walking home. If you discover a nick or bare spot on the insulation of an otherwise good

Try not to use a cigarette lighter or matches to heat-shrink tubing. This heat gun makes the heating process much easier, safer, and less time consuming than other methods. Simply plug it in and press the on/off switch when you want heat. Turn it off when you are done. Just be sure that you do not inadvertently point it toward something flammable.

wire, you can typically wrap the bare spot with a couple of passes of electrical tape to prevent the wire from shorting out. In some situations, you may choose to use electrical tape to tie adjacent wires together so that you don't have the head of a wire tie getting caught if you are pulling a length of wire through the vehicle.

If and when you do use electrical tape, make sure that the surface to be taped is as clean as possible and avoid touching the sticky side of the tape. When you are pulling tape tightly around whatever you are taping, ease up on the tension slightly as you approach the end, as this will help to prevent the tape from pulling loose.

Wire Ties

Wire ties (more commonly known as zip ties) are designed as a quick, easy, and affordable way to tie electrical wires together in a bundle. One end of the wire tie has a square head with internal teeth that allows the opposite end of the tie to be pulled through one way to tighten but not loosen. After pulling the wire tie tight around the wires, the rest of the tie can be cut off with a pair of side cutters. By installing wire ties uniformly every 3 to 6 inches, your bundles of wires will quickly look more organized. Wire ties are available in a variety of lengths and colors (to complement or clash with your paint scheme, as desired).

Test Light

Test lights are a good piece of test equipment to have in your toolbox, especially if you do not have a test meter (more on test meters later). Test lights are inexpensive and can be used to diagnose some pretty basic wiring problems quite easily. Those problems being: is this terminal getting power or will this point serve as a ground? While those questions are very basic, sometimes those basic questions are exactly the questions that need to be asked—and answered correctly.

With one end that looks like an ice pick, a small light bulb, and a length of wire terminated by an alligator clip, a test light can tell you accurately if current is passing through a particular point. It will not be able to tell you how much current, but it will tell you if current is passing through it. Sometimes that is all you really need to know. Simply connect the alligator clip to a known ground and probe the circuit with the pointed end. If the circuit is switched on and current is flowing through it, the light will illuminate. If the light does not illuminate, there is no current, or the ground is not adequate. You may need to clean grease, paint, or debris away from your ground point in order to obtain an adequate ground. Likewise, you can find a good ground by clipping the alligator clamp onto a known power source and probe with the pointed end of the test light until the light illuminates.

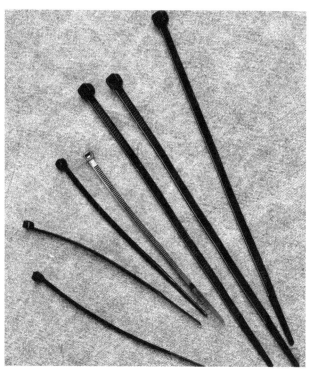

If you look close enough, you will see that wire ties are serrated. This works with a one-way ratchet design within the knob end of the wire tie to allow you to pull the tie tight and not loosen. When you have tied up the wires and pulled them tight, simply cut off the excess tie wire for a clean installation.

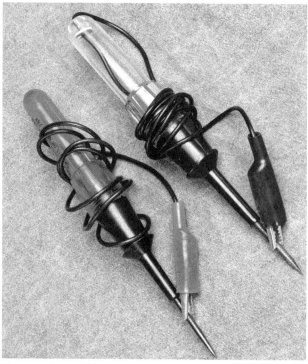

The most basic piece of electrical diagnostic equipment is the test light. The version with the red handle illuminates when the alligator clip is clamped onto a ground source and the probe contacts a wire or terminal that has current (power) flowing through it. While this will tell if you have a complete circuit (power and ground), if the ground is not adequate, it will not illuminate. The improved test meter with the clear housing will have one light that indicates a circuit is grounded and another that indicates if power is flowing through the probed point.

Test Meter

If your electrical wiring experience is limited to making an emergency repair, you most likely will not require a test meter. If that is the case, you probably are not reading this book anyway. While you do not have to be an electrical engineer to use a test meter by any means, the test meter (also called a multimeter) will most likely be able to provide more information than you can digest.

My relatively inexpensive Craftsman digital multimeter will measure ohms, volts DC, volts AC, and battery voltage. The operator simply turns a dial to what is to be measured and then probes the circuitry with the power and ground probes. The resulting information is then displayed on the digital readout. As you can imagine, this is much more valuable when you are trying to diagnose an electrical problem than just knowing if the circuit is receiving power or not. Knowing if there is a voltage drop or not enough amps to power a particular device will help pinpoint the actual problem.

Diagnostic Tool (OBD-I/OBD-II)

This is the computerized scanner tool that reads OBD (onboard diagnostics) systems. As a major effort to meet Environmental Protection Agency (EPA) emission standards, auto manufacturers began using electronics to control engine functions and diagnose engine problems in the 1970s and 1980s. In the mid-1990s, a second generation of this standard, known as OBD-II, was introduced. This newer standard provides diagnostic control over the entire electrical system of the vehicle. Refer to "Electronic Control Module/ Electronic Control Unit," page 70.

A standardization of connector plugs and diagnostic test signals was set by the Society of Automotive Engineers (SAE) in 1988. This gave both professional mechanics and hobbyists the ability to diagnose any OBD-equipped vehicle, as long as they had an OBD scanner.

All passenger cars manufactured since January 1, 1996, have OBD-II systems, with some vehicles being manufactured prior to that time being similarly equipped. Three different protocols (computer speak) are currently being used, with minor variations between the onboard computer and the diagnostic scanner. As electronics in general and computers specifically are being upgraded constantly, it would be prudent to consult with the owner's manual or company website for the diagnostic equipment that you are using for specifics and additional information.

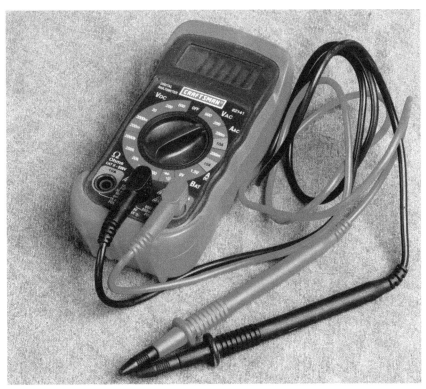

A test meter, multimeter, or volt/ohm meter by any name is your best source for troubleshooting a circuit that is not working as it should. By setting the dial to measure each of a variety of functions, you can determine if the electrical accessory is not getting power, or just isn't getting enough power.

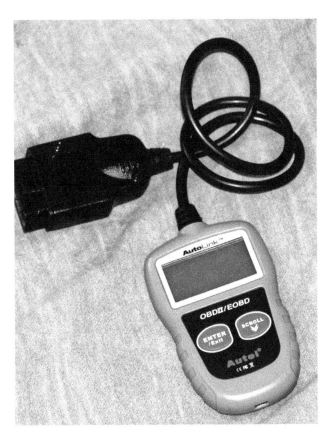

This OBD scanner gets plugged into the OBD plug on the vehicle and then with the engine started the scanner will diagnose the vehicle's electrical problems.

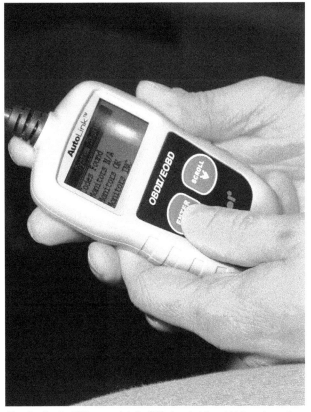

After plugging the OBD scanner into the OBD plug, start the vehicle's engine and follow the instructions for the OBD scanner to diagnose vehicle problems. Many auto parts stores have units such as these so that a customer can determine what repairs need to be done and then replace or clean parts as necessary.

All vehicles equipped with OBD-II systems have a connector mounted where it can be accessed easily from the driver's seat. The diagnostic tool or scanner is plugged into the connector. During the diagnostic process, the vehicle's trouble codes are displayed.

While OBD-II systems have discouraged some hobbyists from working on their vehicle's underhood components, computer-savvy hobbyists have firmly embraced the concept of power-tuning their vehicles by computer. Whether you are striving for better gas mileage, more horsepower, or greener emissions, onboard diagnostics are the key.

Battery Charger

A battery charger is always handy to have in the garage, especially when performing wiring repairs. Rather than put your vehicle's battery and alternator at risk, you can use a battery charger to provide power while testing your electrical system. Be sure to follow the safety precautions listed in the owner's manual when using a battery charger.

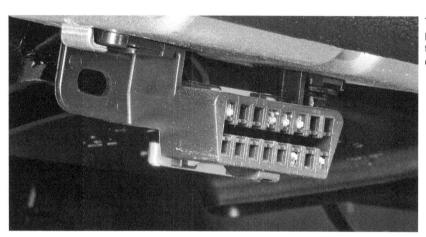

This is the OBD plug on my 2008 Chevrolet Silverado. By plugging an OBD diagnostic tool or scanner into this, a thorough analysis of the vehicle's electrical system can be completed in a matter of minutes.

In addition to charging an ailing battery, a battery charger can be used as the main power source when testing your electrical system after rewiring it. This allows you to check the system, without the possibility of causing damage to the starter, battery, or alternator if something is miswired.

Chapter 2
Ignition and Charging Systems

Okay, now that we have a grasp of the tools and materials involved, it is time to address the ignition and charging systems. Whether you are chasing the cones (formerly black line) at Bonneville, commuting to work, or just cruising Main Street, if the engine doesn't fire off, it is not a good day.

The required basics for making an engine run are fuel, air, and spark, the last of which is ultimately provided by the ignition system. Without it, all the fuel and air you can imagine will not do you any good. While ignition system components can be simple or complex in design, they are relatively simple in theory. Those basic components are an ignition switch, a starter, and ultimately a distributor or magneto. Other components that are commonly part of the ignition circuit, but not an absolute requirement, are master disconnect switches and neutral safety switches.

The charging system is actually a subsystem of the ignition system, and includes the battery(ies) and alternator or generator. Most contemporary passenger vehicles include a charging system, but they may not be included on special-interest vehicles, such as race cars.

IGNITION SYSTEM

The basic concept of the ignition system is to turn the ignition switch so that electrical power is fed to the starter. The starter then engages with the flywheel, rotating the crankshaft and causing the pistons to move up and down, and also causes the distributor (on vehicles so equipped) to send spark to the combustion chamber via the spark plug wires. When this spark is combined with the fuel and air mixture from the induction system, the engine should start.

When power is applied to the solenoid of a starter, the starter motor begins to spin and the starter gear slides outward and engages with the flywheel, causing the flywheel to spin. When you let go of the key in the ignition switch, the starter gear retracts back into the housing of the starter, no longer engaged with the flywheel.

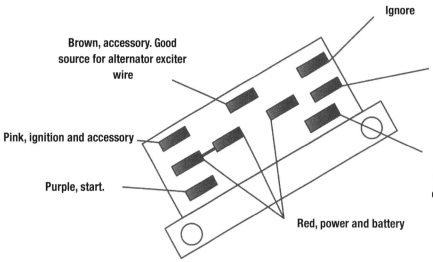

Ignore

Brown, accessory. Good source for alternator exciter wire

Ignore, goes to ground during cranking.

Pink, ignition and accessory

Purple, start.

Physically larger terminal. No power when in accessory position, goes dead during cranking. Good power source for accessories with heavy current draw.

Red, power and battery

Steering columns from General Motors are commonly found in hot rods and other special-interest vehicles. Many of these columns include the column-mount ignition switch that includes terminal connections designed to fit a mating plug, making for easy connections. Be sure the plug's pigtails have sufficient length for splicing if you are buying one of these from the salvage yard or swap meet.

With all of the anti-theft devices on today's vehicles, contemporary ignition switches are actually made of two parts: an electrical switch mechanism and a lock cylinder. Shown is the electrical switch mechanism, to which a lock cylinder would be inserted at the lower right-hand corner.

With the ignition switch in the OFF position, the key slot will typically be slightly back or slightly forward from true vertical. Nothing should be running on the vehicle with the ignition switch in this position, with or without the key in place. The exception to this is that the headlights can be turned on at the headlight switch.

Ignition Switch

At the very simplest application, such as in a race-oriented vehicle, the ignition switch closes the circuit so that the engine can be started. Instead of turning a key to start the vehicle, the driver of a race vehicle may simply flip a number of toggle switches, such as for ignition and fuel pump. Depending on the type of race vehicle, the engine is then either push started, started by a remote starter that is removed from the engine once it starts, or started by a more conventional starter such as the one in your daily driver.

In a conventional factory-built automobile, the ignition system is self-contained within the vehicle, a fact that makes it much more convenient for the ordinary user. Turning the key in the ignition switch begins a chain of events that, when everything is working as designed, all happen automatically to start the engine.

Since there are multiple operating options for the accessories with most any vehicle, the ignition switch has multiple positions, all accessible by simply turning the ignition key. Typically, those positions are OFF, ACCESSORY, IGNITION/RUN, and START. The multiple

The next position forward on the ignition switch is the "ACC" position. The stereo, windshield wipers, horn, power windows, power seats, and other accessories should all operate with the ignition switch in this position. Each accessory will require operation by its own switch, however.

Continuing forward (clockwise) is the IGN/RUN position, which is just prior to the START position. This position of the ignition switch allows the engine and all accessories to run. Unless the engine is running, the ignition switch should not be left in this position for extended periods of time.

positions of the ignition switch (and the correct wiring thereto) is what allows you to listen to the radio without the engine running, requires the engine to be running for the heater to work, and provides enough power to the starter to start the engine.

While the following give the normal or standard situation for each key position, any loose connections or connections that have been rewired incorrectly will give different results. So please bear this in mind when diagnosing or troubleshooting electrical problems. Remember that for an electrical circuit to work properly, it must be a "closed" circuit. If a circuit is "open" either by the position of a switch or a poor connection, that circuit will not operate.

OFF: This is the position that the switch should be in when the ignition key is removed or inserted. Electrically the switch is in an open circuit, so nothing on the vehicle should be running, except for the headlights if they are turned ON at the headlight switch. Note that on some vehicles, an electric fan used to cool the engine may continue to run for some time after the ignition switch is shut off, even if the key is removed from the ignition switch.

ACCESSORY: This position will vary between vehicles, but is typically one step backward or one step forward from the OFF position. When the ignition switch is moved into this position, the accessory circuit closes, allowing the stereo and other accessories to operate. IGNITION/RUN and START circuits are still open.

IGNITION/RUN: This is the position that the ignition key returns to after the engine is started and remains in until the engine is shut off. This will close the IGNITION, ACCESSORY, and heater/AC circuits, allowing the engine and all accessories to run. Simply put, this is the position for when the vehicle is being driven.

START: This is the farthest position from OFF and is used solely to start the engine. When the ignition key is in this position, only the IGNITION and START circuits are closed.

This is a typical GM starter, complete with burned and spliced wires. The black canister portion is the actual starter motor. The smaller shiny cylinder above it is the solenoid and is where the wires connect. The shiny (albeit grungy) portion is where the two mounting bolts go through the starter assembly to the engine block. Below this in the photo is where the gear on the starter motor shaft engages with the flywheel.

Shown is a late-model Ford starter that includes an integral solenoid. Earlier Ford starters used a remote solenoid. Two mounting ears at the base of the housing are for the mounting bolts. Note that the mounting bolts run parallel with the starter, rather than perpendicular as on a GM starter.

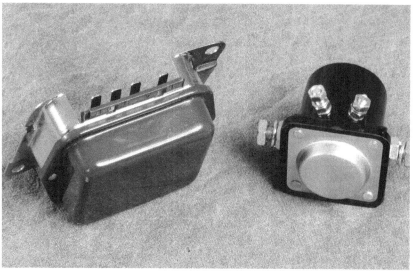

At the left is a voltage regulator and at the right is a solenoid, both for an early Ford. The two small terminals on the solenoid connect to the coil, while the large terminals connect to the battery and the starter.

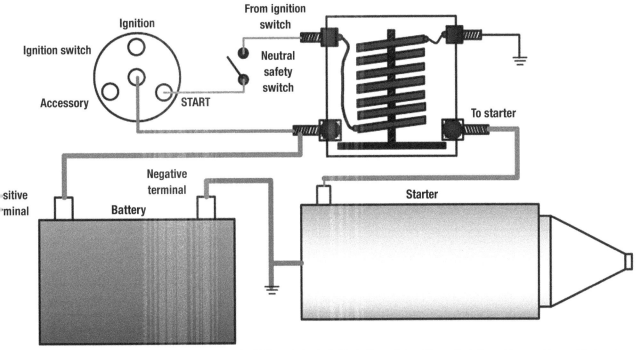

Ignition switch

Ignition

Accessory

START

From ignition switch

Neutral safety switch

To starter

...sitive ...minal

Negative terminal

Battery

Starter

This is an example of a Ford ignition circuit using an external solenoid. The main terminal of the ignition switch and the positive battery cable connect to one of the large lugs on the solenoid. Power goes from the other large lug on the solenoid to the starter. The starter and the negative battery cable both run to ground. The start terminal from the ignition switch runs through a neutral safety switch and then to the positive small terminal on the coil. The negative small terminal on the coil runs to ground.

This position is spring loaded so that the ignition switch will return to the RUN position when released. If the key were to remain in the START position, the starter gear would remain engaged with the flywheel and burn up the starter in the process.

Since the ignition switch actually switches a multitude of components, several wires may be connected to it, whether the switch resides in the steering column or in the dash. Directly or indirectly, depending on make and model, most all accessories are connected to the ignition switch. They are typically operated by their own switch mechanism (on/off, high/low, etc.), but the presence of electrical power is ultimately determined by the ignition switch.

Starters

Automobile starters fall into one of three different styles, with each of Detroit's Big Three claiming its own style. The big difference between the three styles is where the starter solenoid is in relation to the starter itself. On the General Motors style, the solenoid is attached directly to the starter. On the early-Ford style, the solenoid is mounted remotely (typically on the fender or firewall), while the solenoid is integral on later-Ford starters. On the Chrysler style, the solenoid is attached directly to the starter, but is controlled by a relay.

Other than these subtle (yet important when you are replacing) differences, starters are basically the same in that

they are an electric motor. A steel case houses two or four field windings. An armature wound with several windings of copper wire rotates within the field windings. These armature windings connect to a copper commutator that, in turn, connects to the battery and ground as the armature and commutator rotate.

Turning the ignition switch to the START position, thereby energizing the starter, causes electrical current to pass through the field windings and create a magnetic field. Likewise, electrical current passing through the armature

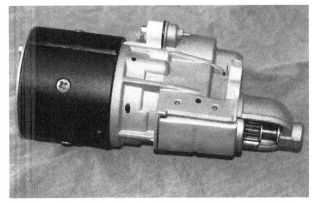

On this later 1970s Chrysler starter, the solenoid is attached directly to the starter, but due to the high current involved, is controlled by a relay.

creates a magnetic field. The magnetic polarity of these fields causes them to attract or repel, causing the armature to rotate. During this rotation, different windings become energized, causing the starter to build up torque. This torque is what causes the engine to turn over.

Two conditions that severely hamper operation of the starter are voltage drop and excessive ambient heat. Since electrical resistance increases as the temperature increases, the electrical circuit must be at its optimum condition in order to compensate. To minimize voltage drop, verify that connections between the starter or solenoid and the battery cable are clean (not corroded) and tightly secured.

It is also imperative that the starter be grounded adequately. The best way to do this is to connect the negative battery cable directly to the engine block. The positive battery cable between the battery and the starter and the negative battery cable must be large enough to carry the required current.

One method of eliminating the hot start problem is to install a 30-amp relay in the ignition circuit between the ignition switch and the starter. Extreme cold weather also plays havoc with starting systems that are not in optimum condition; however, this is due more to the sluggishness of oil in the engine being allowed to get cold and become thicker than an actual electrical problem.

CHARGING SYSTEMS

While the battery is what serves as the power source for starting the vehicle, it also provides power to run the air conditioning, stereo, lights, and all of the other electrically powered components that we have grown to depend on. Since we expect the engine to start and all of these creature comforts to operate the next time we get behind the wheel, the battery requires a method of being conveniently recharged. This is the reason for having an alternator or generator.

Batteries

Automotive batteries serve three basic purposes: to produce electric power, to store that power, and to regulate that power. To produce electrical power, batteries are made up of plates made of lead alloys suspended in a solution made up of sulfuric acid and water. When suspended in this sulfuric

The best place for your vehicle's battery is in the vehicle, but if you do remove it for any of a number of reasons, do not simply set it on a concrete garage floor. Doing so may cause the battery to quickly discharge. If you do set it on the floor, set it on a couple of strips of wood so that it will still be fully charged when you are ready to use it again. Many people will claim that this is an old wives tale, but some still agree with the practice. Evidently this concern started when battery cases were made of porous materials, such as tar-lined wooden boxes. The batteries would leak, thus discharging in the process. Modern batteries are constructed of hard rubber or polypropylene, and therefore seal better.

When it comes to storing car batteries, the following is what you really need to know. All batteries will discharge a bit while they are in storage, no matter how they are stored. You should keep the battery clean and in a cool location while it is being stored, as heat is as much of a cause of battery discharge as anything else. Simply put, the higher the ambient temperature, the quicker the battery will discharge. As for a car battery and a concrete floor, if the battery does leak battery acid onto the concrete, the acid will begin to eat into the concrete.

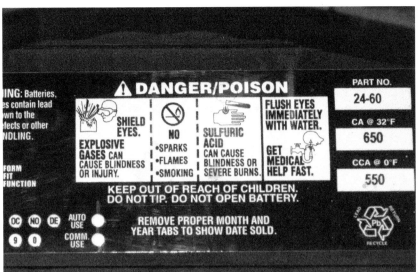

This label on the top of the battery includes the CCA (550 in this instance) for this battery. It also provides safety precautions and date of purchase information for warranty situations.

acid and water mix, positive plates constructed from lead peroxide and negative plates constructed from sponge lead create an electrical current as part of the chemical reaction.

As an electrical storage device, batteries are rated by cold cranking amps (CCA) and reserve capacity. The CCA is the number of amps the battery is able to deliver after being chilled to 0 degrees Fahrenheit, and then placed under a load for 30 seconds while providing a consistent 7.2 volts. A larger rating (typically between 500 and 750) indicates that the battery can put out more power to start your vehicle. This rating is provided to compare batteries for use between warmer and colder climates. The reserve capacity is the length of time a fully charged battery can be discharged at 25 amps without allowing voltage to drop below 1.75 volts in any individual cell. This rating compares batteries in a situation where the charging system has failed.

The electrical voltage and current fluctuate as the engine rpm increases or decreases or when the electrical demand increases or decreases. Your vehicle's battery is able to stabilize voltage and minimize spikes during these fluctuations. As an example, if it were not for the buffering ability of the battery, turning off the air conditioning (decreasing the electrical demand) could cause a voltage spike that could damage your stereo.

While batteries are capable of producing electrical energy, they also give off hydrogen gas, which is quite explosive. For this simple reason, it is imperative to eliminate cigarettes, flames, or sparks from the vicinity of the battery. This is especially important when the battery is being charged or is under a load. This is also why the last cable to be connected when jump starting a vehicle is the negative cable to the vehicle being jumped (the one with the "dead" battery). To further remove the potential of sparks from the battery, connect this negative battery cable to the engine block or vehicle frame, rather than to the battery.

After starting the engine on my 2008 Chevrolet Silverado, the voltmeter reads about 14.5 volts. It dropped a bit after letting it run for a while with no accessories turned ON. Letting the engine idle or revving up the engine has no significance on how much voltage the alternator puts out.

After starting the engine and turning on the stereo and the air conditioning, the voltage begins to creep up a bit as demand increases. If additional electrically operated accessories were in use, the voltmeter would have read somewhat higher. On a vehicle with a standard 12-volt electrical system, the voltmeter normally reads between 11 and 17 volts.

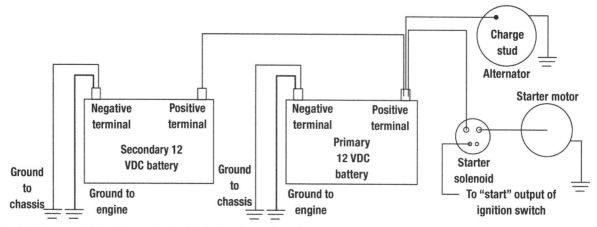

When installing a second battery, the new charge lead to the alternator should be at least a 4-gauge wire. Both batteries should be grounded to the engine block or transmission, as well as to the vehicle's chassis. Secondary battery should also be the same brand and type as the primary battery and as close in age as possible.

During normal use, the positive terminal of the battery will be connected to the starter. The negative terminal of the battery should be grounded to the engine block or transmission case.

Generators and Alternators

Generators and alternators serve the same basic purpose of recharging the battery, so you will use one or the other, but not both. They are similar in construction, but by design they are significantly different and therefore offer different characteristics. Generators and alternators are similar to a starter motor, as they are made up of field coils, magnetic fields, and armatures wound with windings. Like most other electrical devices, for either of these to work correctly, a generator or an alternator must be grounded adequately.

Generators: Older vehicles (manufactured approximately 1960 and earlier) used generators to recharge the battery with DC (direct current) voltage. A regulator is used inline between the generator and the battery to control current and voltage output.

An advantage of a generator is that the field wires are wrapped around a permanent magnet, therefore there is always some amount of magnetic field. This is part of the reason an older vehicle with a dead battery could be push started. Once the vehicle was rolling, the generator would begin creating DC power.

Some disadvantages of generators are that they do not produce as much power as alternators, they require more rpm to produce power, and generator brushes (contacts) tend to wear out quickly.

In this nostalgic, period-perfect '40 Ford coupe, the engine is a Ford flathead that includes a generator (lower left of photo) to keep the battery charged. When compared to a modern-day alternator, a generator is approximately two or three times as long.

In this under-construction '40 Ford coupe, the black painted generator is located top center between the radiator hoses. The construction of a generator allows it to maintain a magnetic field, so this car could be started easily by pushing it or rolling it down a hill should its battery die. Just be sure to turn the ignition switch to the ON position first.

Late-model alternators are an improvement over generators from an engineering standpoint, as they require less maintenance by design. This particular alternator has a vented case that allows it to dissipate heat quickly and effectively.

Alternators: Modern vehicles typically use alternators to recharge the battery with AC (alternating current) voltage. Diodes, typically mounted within the frame of the alternator, convert the AC voltage to DC voltage that is used in automobiles. While most contemporary alternators use an internal voltage regulator, a regulator (internal or external) must be used with an alternator. Electrical current output is self-regulating with an alternator, however.

Advantages of alternators are several when compared to a generator, with the latter being used mostly for period-piece restorations. Alternators require little if any maintenance and are able to produce vast amounts of power. The bulk of that power can also be made at a relatively low speed, but alternators can spin at greater speed without suffering damage.

A disadvantage (and this is slight) is that alternators do not contain permanent magnets, so they do not have that ever-present magnetic field within that generators have. What this actually means is that without being energized from some other power source, an alternator will not produce power on its own, regardless of how fast you spin it.

When working around an alternator, you must remember that the wire connecting to the back of the alternator is hot all the time. So, if you inadvertently touch a wrench or screwdriver onto the alternator charge stud and a suitable ground, sparks will fly. Not only will sparks fly, you may possibly damage other components such as the starter, distributor, or alternator itself. You must also remember that the wire connected to the back of the alternator must be large enough to carry the full output of the alternator. For the most part, this will require an 8-gauge wire or larger (which means it will be numerically smaller).

Alternators are rated by their amperage output, but if you do not require the extra amps, you will never see the benefit. Engine rpm has a direct impact on an alternator's output rating, so an alternator rated at 100 amps will not put out any more power than one rated at 50 or 60 if the extra amps are not required. Since it is rare that all electrical circuits will be used at the same time, you should determine the total amount of current required during full-load conditions, and then purchase an alternator with a similar rating.

Using an alternator instead of a generator is a fairly simple choice, as the former is clearly an overall improvement. If it wasn't, why would all major manufacturers of automobiles use them? The not-so-obvious choice is whether or not to use a three-wire or a one-wire alternator.

Three-Wire Alternator: A three-wire alternator has three connection points to the ignition and charging systems and is therefore able to provide more accurate information to your vehicle's electrical monitoring system. These electrical connections are the charge (or output) stud, ignition sense, and battery sense.

The charge or output stud is common to both the three-wire alternator and the one-wire alternator and is located on the back of the alternator. Power to the alternator typically comes directly from the positive terminal on the battery or from the fuse panel. By placing a fusible link inline between these two connections, possible damage to the battery and accessories caused by a faulty voltage regulator can be prevented.

The ignition sense connection is connected to the IGN/RUN terminal on the ignition switch and simply lets the alternator know when the vehicle's engine is running. A ballast resistor is typically located inline between the ignition switch and the alternator. The job of the ballast resistor is to absorb some of the "extra" voltage that is passed between the ignition switch and the ignition sense terminal of the

At the upper right of the back of this alternator is the charge stud, which is electrically hot all the time. While the alternator is a GM three-wire unit, it is being used with a Ford V-6 engine due to space limitations. Some auto manufacturers use a rubber boot to cover the charge stud to prevent accidental shorts.

alternator, as too much voltage can cause damage to the sensing circuit. An alternative to the use of a ballast resistor is to install a light (also called an idiot light) between the two connections to bleed off some of this extra voltage.

The battery sense lead connects to the fuse panel and provides power requirement feedback to the alternator. Effectively, this tells the alternator to make more or less power, depending on the electrical demands of the system at the time.

One-Wire Alternator: A one-wire alternator monitors voltage at the output stud, but with only one input source, it cannot be as accurate as a three-wire alternator. With only one connection, however, the one-wire alternator is easier to install or replace.

With the GM one-wire alternator requiring only one electrical connection to be made to the charge stud on the back of the unit, installation or replacement is simple.

This is an older-style GM three-wire alternator, albeit with a serpentine belt pulley. At the top, back of the alternator are two terminals, while the third wire would connect to the charge stud on the back that is not seen in this photo. For the most part, V-belt and serpentine belt pulleys are interchangeable from one alternator to another within the vehicle manufacturer.

Typically mounted on the firewall by one bolt, this is what a ballast resistor looks like while in use (rectangular white piece). With the two electrical terminals, the ballast resistor is easily installed inline between the ignition switch and the alternator.

While starting an engine, the system voltage drops considerably. So, to allow the engine to start, the ignition system must be designed to operate on this lower voltage. Once the engine is started, however, the normal operating voltage returns and would overload the ignition system if not controlled by a ballast resistor.

In automotive applications, a master disconnect switch is designed to be installed inline of the positive battery cable between the battery and starter. The battery cable simply connects to the master disconnect switch with ring terminals, with one terminal running to the battery and the other running to the starter. When the switch is in the OFF position, there should not be any electrical current reaching the engine.

With the GM one-wire alternator requiring only one electrical connection to be made to the charge stud on the back of the unit, installation or replacement is simple.

For a non-gearhead person, the three-wire alternator works well because it can more accurately monitor the electrical system. For an auto enthusiast or someone who is better versed in vehicle diagnostics and maintenance, the one-wire alternator is a much simpler design, necessitating two fewer wires to clutter the engine compartment.

OTHER COMPONENTS

A couple of other components are commonly found within the ignition system but are not mandatory on all vehicles. These are a master disconnect switch and a neutral safety switch.

Master Disconnect Switch

A master disconnect switch is not required on any vehicle but is typically installed as a theft deterrent or sometimes as a safety mechanism on race-bred vehicles. Sometimes referred to as a kill switch, a master disconnect switch opens or "kills" all electrical circuits, shutting down all electrical power to the vehicle.

To work properly on a street-driven vehicle, the master disconnect switch should be installed inline between the battery and the starter. This will prevent the engine from starting and therefore will prevent most accessories from working as well, although preventing the engine from running is the primary purpose of the kill switch. On a race-oriented vehicle, sanctioning bodies may have specific requirements for which circuits (ignition, fuel pump, and so on) must be included within the circuit protected by a master kill switch. It is then typically mounted in a specific location outside of the vehicle so that safety crews can quickly locate it and shut off electricity to the vehicle in the case of a mishap.

It would seem obvious that this type of switch should be positioned within easy reach of the driver, so that it can be turned ON easily when you are simply going for a drive in your late model vehicle, or can be turned OFF easily (and quickly) if your race vehicle has gone askew. Many master disconnect switches are two-position rotary switches that simply have an ON and OFF position. If the battery cable

Mounted near the base of the column shifter steering column, this stock neutral safety switch in a '68 Chevrolet pickup has four terminals. Two of the terminals ("park start" and "neutral start") must be connected to the ignition circuit. One of the other terminals is for the backup lights and is powered when the shifter is put into reverse.

On this aftermarket shifter, a ball fits into a detent and acts as a pressure switch when the shifter is in PARK or NEUTRAL, allowing the vehicle to be started. In any other shifter positions, the ball is not pushed in completely, leaving an open (non-start) circuit. Ignition wires would connect to the two electrical terminals with ring connectors at the right of the photo.

runs beneath the floor and under the passenger compartment, the switch can easily be installed in the floor, just under the front of the driver's seat. This makes it convenient for the driver, yet somewhat unobtrusive to legroom or to a typically crowded dash panel. An alternative to this might be a two-position toggle switch that could be mounted on the dash, as it would be somewhat smaller than the rotary-style switch. Of course, if you are using this type of switch primarily as a theft deterrent, your switch location may be located anywhere you want it.

Some master disconnect switches are available with an auxiliary terminal that allows for a power connection of a car alarm, while still shutting off power to all other circuits.

Neutral Safety Switch

While a neutral safety switch is not a required component to an ignition system, it is a good idea. This is the mechanism that allows a vehicle's engine to start only when the automatic transmission is in PARK or NEUTRAL, or a standard transmission-equipped vehicle to start only when the vehicle is in NEUTRAL or the clutch is depressed. If a vehicle's engine is able to start while the transmission is in gear, results could be (and have been) catastrophic.

Neutral safety switches vary from manufacturer, but will be designed to activate based on the position of the shifter linkage. Located electrically between the ignition switch and the starter solenoid, the neutral safety switch typically has two electrical contacts. One contact is for "park start" and the other being "neutral start." On some vehicles, the neutral safety switch may be part of a larger switch that also controls backup lights. If you are rewiring a vehicle and do not know

which terminals apply to the neutral safety switch, you can determine them by the following procedure:

Clip the ground connection of a test light to a good ground. With the ignition switch OFF, you should be able to probe terminals until the test light illuminates. That terminal will be common (hot). Then turn the ignition switch on and place the gear selector in PARK. Then probe the terminals until the test light illuminates. That terminal should be "park start." Then place the gear selector in neutral and repeat the probe test until the test light illuminates again. The terminal that lights up should be the "neutral start."

You may have to actually put the key in the START position to get continuity with the two start terminals. If so, get someone to hold the key in start while you probe. You should also disconnect the wire from the "S" terminal on the starter solenoid so the engine does not start. The remaining terminal should be REVERSE, but you can verify that by placing the gear selector into reverse with the key just in the *on* position and use the test light. PARK, NEUTRAL, and REVERSE should show continuity with common when the gear selector is in the position for each.

Ground (Return Path)

Just as essential in an electrical system as power is an adequate ground (also called a return path). Quite simply, if you provide power to an electrical accessory, but do not ground that accessory, it will not work. Knowing and accepting this is every bit as important as knowing Ohm's or Kirchhoff's laws. Some components won't work at all if not grounded, while others will work sporadically.

For years, vehicle manufacturers have commonly used the vehicle's chassis as a ground for the starter circuit by connecting the negative battery cable between the negative post of the battery and the chassis. Being made of fairly heavy metal, the vehicle's chassis worked well as a ground when it was new. As the vehicle aged, however, and accumulated rust, dirt, grease, and grime, it was no longer the good conductor that it had been. Also, as unibody vehicle construction came into being, the one-time heavy vehicle chassis was on its way out. So, whether you are working on an older vehicle or a newer one, for the reasons above it makes more sense to ground the battery to the engine block or transmission (typically a bellhousing or transmission-mount bolt) by way of a large battery cable. The engine is a fairly heavy piece of metal and is not subject to quite as much dirt and debris as the undercarriage, so it does serve as an adequate ground.

For all of the other electrical accessories in your vehicle to work, they must be grounded also. Now we know that the engine provides a suitable ground, but it is not always feasible to connect ground wires from every light and accessory to the engine block. For this purpose, a ground strap or wire (6- or 8-gauge) should be run between the vehicle's chassis and engine block, grounding the vehicle's chassis in the process. This will allow the chassis to serve as a ground source for items such as the fuel pump, electric fan, and horn. Likewise, a ground strap or wire (10-gauge) should be run between the body and engine block, grounding the body in the process. The body's sheet metal will provide convenient grounding locations for lights, gauges, and other accessories. Providing a return path in this method has been done by manufacturers for years and works well on steel-bodied vehicles that are well maintained. However, as the sheet-metal components begin to rust or simply collect roadway grime on their underside, grounding issues can begin to appear.

Since fiberglass is not a good conductor, there is no need to connect a fiberglass body (such as a reproduction hot rod or kit car) itself to a chassis or engine ground. Components inside the body, such as gauges, stereo, and lights, still need to be grounded to some steel portion of the vehicle. Rather than lights or accessories grounding through their mounting to a steel body, a separate ground wire must be used.

A better method than what the vehicle manufacturers' use is required on fiberglass-bodied vehicles and works well on steel-bodied vehicles as well. Begin by grounding the battery directly to the engine block or transmission and adding a ground strap from this same point over to the chassis. Now determine suitable centralized locations near the front, rear, and interior of the vehicle to mount grounding studs. A 10-32 x 3/4 stainless steel screw, a 10-32 brass nut, and a 10-32 wing nut will be required for each ground stud. You can use different sized hardware if desired, but this size is suitable without being obnoxiously large. Drill the appropriate size hole for the hardware you are using in the vehicle's chassis at the front and rear and in the interior near the dash. Run 12-gauge wire from the battery to each grounding stud and terminate the wire with a no. 10 ring terminal. Insert the stainless steel screw through the ring terminal, into the hole in the chassis (or dash), and secure with the brass nut. You now have a convenient ground location for your lights and accessories. Terminate each ground wire with a ring terminal, and then slide it over the ground stud and secure with the wing nut. Several ground wires can be connected to a common grounding stud. This method will prevent you from having multiple ground wires running throughout the length of the vehicle and will also eliminate sporadic electrical problems caused by improper grounding.

Using a no. 4-gauge battery cable, the negative terminal of the trunk-mounted battery is connected to the engine block with a bolt on the front of the block (just in front and below the valve cover).

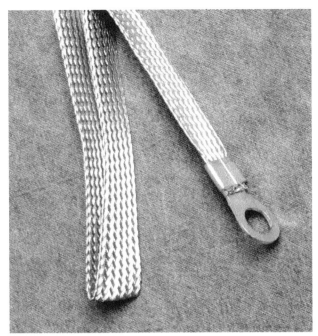

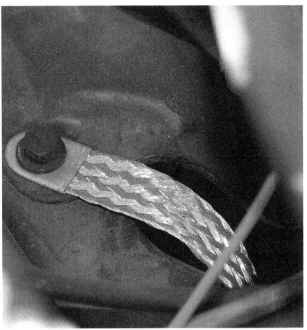

While a heavy battery cable should be used between the negative battery post and the engine block, a braided ground strap can be used between the engine block and vehicle chassis or the engine block and the body sheet metal. By tying the body sheet metal and vehicle's chassis to the ground source that the battery is connected to, the body and chassis can be used as a convenient ground source for other electrical devices.

Since the engine block is mounted with rubber or urethane between the motor mounts, the engine is insulated from the vehicle's chassis. This calls for a heavy ground strap to be installed between the engine block and the chassis. The ground strap shown mounts to the chassis at one of the bolt-on motor mounts and on the opposite end to the engine block where the negative battery cable is also connected.

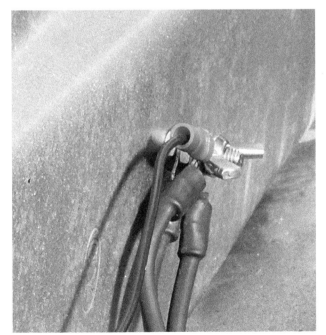

By locating a 10-32 x 3/4 stainless steel screw, a 10-32 brass nut, and a 10-32 wing nut strategically around the vehicle, you can easily establish central locations for a suitable ground. This ground stud has been inserted through a hole in the inner fender sheet metal and is secured in place by a nut (no need for a grommet in this case since it is a ground stud [screw opposed to wire]). After grounding this stud by connecting it to the negative post of the battery, ground wires for accessories can be connected with a ring terminal and secured by the wing nut.

From each ground stud located throughout the vehicle, route the ground wires to the negative post of the battery. Connect them with ring terminals sized to fit the clamping bolt of the negative battery cable. Each ground stud can be connected independently or combined with another as desired.

Chapter 3
Lighting Systems

Electrically speaking, lighting systems are really pretty simple. They require bulbs and a mounting mechanism, power, ground, and a method of switching ON and OFF, but little else. Unlike the ignition system, you don't have to be concerned with determining if a problem is lack of fuel, air, or spark to the combustion chamber or an electrical problem. Other than collision damage, the most typical of lighting problems is having an inadequate ground, with a burned-out light bulb being a distant second.

EXTERIOR OR RUNNING LIGHTS

Exterior vehicle lighting includes headlights, taillights, and brake lights on most all street-driven vehicles. Additional exterior lighting includes front and rear turn signals, parking lights, clearance lights, foglights, and driving lights. Items from this last group may or may not be on your vehicle, depending on its vintage and type. An authentically restored Ford Model A will not have turn signals but may have cowl lights (a type of clearance light). An off-road vehicle may have several sets of driving and foglights but may not have parking lights. As long as you meet the requirements of your local licensing authority, optional exterior lighting is up to you.

Headlights

In general, headlights are controlled by a headlight switch that is mounted somewhere on the dash and a dimmer switch that is mounted on the floor (older vehicles) or mounted on the steering column (on most newer vehicles). The headlight switch may be a push-pull type or a rotary type or rocker style. While operation differs accordingly, wiring is basically the same for either type. With a push-pull switch, pulling the light switch knob all the way out typically turns the headlights ON, while pushing it in all the way turns the lights OFF. There may be an in-between position that turns ON only the parking lights. With a rotary-type switch, turning the knob fully clockwise turns the headlights ON, while turning it fully counterclockwise turns the lights OFF. Rocker-style headlight switches will usually be a single pole, single throw type, meaning that the headlights will be ON in one position and OFF in the other.

Many newer vehicles use a rotary switch that has an automatic position. This feature typically includes daytime running lamps that are ON whenever the engine is running, but automatically turns the headlights and taillights ON whenever the ambient lighting is below a predetermined level. Perhaps the biggest advantage of this feature is that it allows the headlights to stay ON for a predetermined amount of time after you exit the vehicle and then turns them OFF automatically.

The dimmer switch, whether mounted on the floor or steering column, is a single-pole, double-throw switch that determines if the headlights are on high beam or low beam. For more on switches, refer to Chapter 4. The dimmer switch does not turn the headlights ON or OFF, it merely controls which circuit (high-beam or low-beam) the electricity follows through the headlight.

Wiring the headlights is done by running a power wire (12-gauge or larger) from the fuse panel to the input terminal of the headlight switch. In addition to an input terminal, the headlight switch will have separate terminals for headlights, taillights, courtesy lights, and parking lights. From the headlight terminal, run a wire to the input terminal of the dimmer switch. From the low-beam terminal of the dimmer switch, run a wire to each low-beam lamp. From the high-beam terminal of the dimmer switch, run a wire to each high-beam lamp. Between the dimmer switch and each of the low-beam and high-beam lamps, the wire can go to one lamp and then to the other lamp or can be run to a location in between each lamp and then split to run in opposite directions to each lamp.

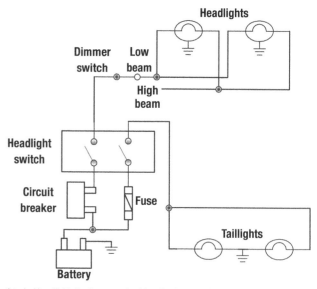

A typical headlight circuit uses a circuit breaker between the battery power and the headlight switch to protect the headlights. A circuit breaker is often part of the headlight switch. A fuse located between the battery power and the headlight switch protects the taillights and parking lights.

HEADLIGHT AIMING

Have you ever passed a vehicle whose headlights were shining up in the trees, or on the pavement only a couple of feet in front of the car? Worse yet, met a car whose low beams were still directed right in your eyes? Proper headlight aiming will make nighttime driving much safer and more enjoyable. Having run wire to the headlights is only part of the way to having proper lights. A critical part of installing headlights is actually getting them pointed in the correct direction. While aiming your headlights and wiring them are two different things, your headlights may not be aimed as accurately as they should be.

To check the aim of the headlights on your vehicle, you need to have approximately 35 to 40 feet of uniformly sloped driving area and a wall. The driving surface does not have to be level, as long as it is consistently flat, so your driveway and garage door may work. With the front of the vehicle parked from 2 to 3 feet from the wall (or garage door), turn the low-beam headlights ON. With a pencil or tape, outline the bright spots on the wall.

Park the vehicle 2 or 3 feet from the wall or garage door. Measure 25 feet back from the front wheels to where they will need to be for the next step. Note that in all actuality, dusk, dawn, or in the shade would be a much easier situation to do this in, but for the photos, I used the available light.

Turn the low-beam headlights ON, and then mark the location of the light beams on the garage door with masking tape. After marking the location of the light beams, back the vehicle 25 feet. The top of the low-beam shining on the wall should be no higher than the top marks on the wall, or lower than the center of the original area. If the lights are outside of those parameters, adjust them accordingly and retest until they are dialed in.

Now back the vehicle straight back to about 25 feet away from the same wall. Again, turn the low beam headlights ON. The top of the low beam shining on the wall should be no higher than the top marks on the wall, or lower than the center of the original area.

Adjust as necessary and repeat the aiming procedure until it is dialed in. By aiming the low beams in this manner, the high beams of a two-headlight system will automatically be properly adjusted.

On my '68 Chevy C10 pickup, and on most other vehicles, there are two headlight adjustment screws. Typically, one is located above the top center of the headlight and another to one side. The first allows for up-and-down adjustment, while the second one provides adjustment left and right.

HID (high intensity discharge) lights, also known as Xenon headlamps, were introduced in Europe in 1991 and became available in the United States two years later. The Xenon gas used in these metal halide lamps is what provides the bluish tint that typify these lights. The blue tint coincides with a specific light temperature (between 10,000 and 12,000K), but other colors, such as yellow (3,000K) or white (between 4,300 and 8,000K) are also available. Unlike conventional automotive headlamps, HID lamp bulbs require a ballast and an internal or external igniter. Current to the bulb is controlled by the ballast, while the igniter works in

similar fashion as a spark plug to ionize the Xenon gas. HID lamps provide significantly greater amounts of usable light for the driver, but face criticism that they negatively impair the vision of oncoming drivers.

Available as OEM options on more domestic vehicles each year, HID headlamps are also available as aftermarket upgrades. For service questions or installation, you should refer to a vehicle-specific service manual or the installation instructions for the specific kit you are installing.

Each of the headlight bulbs will need to be grounded for them to work properly. For the high-beam indicator to

The various lights can be wired to operate differently, but from the factory, the parking lights and side marker lights are typically ON and the headlights OFF when the headlight switch is pulled out or rotated to the first position. The parking lights would flash on the appropriate side when the turn signals are activated.

When the headlight switch is moved to the second position, the headlights turn ON, along with the side marker lights. The parking lights then go OFF.

function, it will need to be connected via a wire from the high-beam side of the dimmer switch. Most aftermarket wiring kits will include this wire, but you can simply splice into the high-beam side of the headlight wiring if you are creating your own wiring harness. Remember that the high-beam indicator light will also require its own ground.

Parking Lights

Parking lights may often use the same bulbs or light fixture as the front turn signals, but they are wired as part of a separate circuit. To wire the parking lights, run a 16-gauge wire from the parking light terminal on the headlight switch to each of the parking lights. Also verify that each parking light is grounded either through the housing or via a separate ground wire. Wiring parking lights is similar to wiring the headlights, except the parking light circuit does not use a dimmer switch.

Aftermarket wiring kits for vehicles that have side marker lights will typically include wires to power those lights. If those separate wires are not available, however, the side marker lights can be added to the circuit that includes the parking lights. For instance, a wire could run from the parking light terminal on the headlight switch to

Side marker lights are typically wired into the headlight and taillight circuit if they are even illuminated. An option would be to wire them as part of the turn signal circuit. Some side marker lights do not have provisions for a light bulb and are merely reflectors. On this vehicle, the side marker lights are wired so that they are illuminated when the headlights and taillights are ON.

Side marker lights are not as common as they used to be, as they are now incorporated within the headlight or taillight that wrap around the front or rear corners of the vehicle. Where side marker lights are present, they are often merely reflectors. Depending on how the housing is designed, adding light may simply be a matter of installing a light socket and running wires to it.

a point near the front of the vehicle. From this point, the wire would split off in two directions (driver's side and passenger's side) and each branch would connect to the parking light and the side marker light. Refer to "Turn-Signal Lights," page 47.

Taillights: Taillights are wired using the same methods used on the parking lights, except that the wires run from the taillight terminal on the headlight switch to each of the vehicle's two taillights and rear side marker lights if used. Remember that these wires are for the taillights and rear side marker lights only, and therefore should not be connected to a third brake light. Refer to "Turn-Signal Lights," page 47.

Brake Lights: While the brake lights often use the same bulb as the taillights, they are part of a different circuit. A 14-gauge or larger wire runs from the fuse panel to the brake light switch. This provides power to the brake light circuit

whenever the key is in the ACC or RUN position. Note that on some older vehicles (pre-1960), stepping on the brake pedal will illuminate the brake lights with or without a key in the ignition switch. If the vehicle you are working on falls into this category, you should refer to a vehicle-specific service manual. A second output wire from the brake light switch connects to the turn signal switch, the other works as a turn signal. The turn signal switch splits the circuit when the turn signal indicator is activated. The circuit is closed and the brake lights are activated when the brake light switch is activated. This is done by one of three different types of brake light switch, all of which are open until the brake pedal is depressed.

Two of the brake light switch types (button and lever) are similar, as they require a mechanical interface between the brake pedal arm and the switch itself. In either case, the brake light switch is mounted so that when the brake pedal is depressed, the brake pedal arm pushes the button

While the actual clear bulbs are difficult to see in this photo of the taillight in my Silverado, it is easy enough to see the three individual sockets behind the prismatic lens. Both the upper and lower bulbs are wired to operate as brake, tail-, and turn-signal lights. Some vehicles would use separate bulbs for each function.

This CHMSL (center high-mounted stop lamp) includes a cargo lamp and is mounted above the rear window of this pickup truck. Mounting a brake light in the center (laterally) of the vehicle and higher than the rearmost brake lights gives following drivers a significantly better chance of seeing brake lights in front of them.

or lever and closes the circuit. Some brake light switches are designed just the opposite, however: The button or arm is at rest as long as the brake pedal is against it, but the spring-loaded button or arm activates when the brake pedal is pushed away from it.

The third type of brake light switch is a pressure type and is activated by increased fluid pressure when the brake pedal is depressed. Once positioned correctly, the mechanical switch requires no maintenance and is therefore the common type among OEMs. Hot rodders and custom car builders are the typical users of the pressure brake light switch. When using a pressure brake light switch, it is highly recommended to use an electrical relay in the circuit. If a relay is not used,

the switch will most likely fail without warning, resulting in no brake lights. This is the common cause of failure with this type of switch, although low brake fluid could cause a similar result.

Turn-Signal Lights: Wiring for turn signals is usually made up in a relatively short pigtail (a group of wires with similar endpoints), as power must run from the fuse panel to the turn-signal mechanism located on the steering column. Commonly, a plug is then used to connect the multiple turn-signal terminals on the fuse panel to the appropriate wires within the steering column–mounted signal mechanism. This allows for the entire turn-signal circuit to be disconnected at

On a button-style brake light switch, the switch must be mounted so that the movement of the brake pedal during braking depresses the white button. The brake light switch can be mounted in a hole in the firewall or a bracket and secured by tightening the two silver-colored nuts along the shaft of the switch body. A wire from each of the two male terminals on the end of the switch connects to the brake light circuit.

On a lever-style brake light switch, a portion of the switch fits onto the brake pedal arm and therefore moves when the brake pedal is depressed. The other portion of the switch is physically connected to the first through a common pivot point but is in a fixed location. As the brake pedal is moved, electrical contacts between both portions align, activating the brake light switch.

On a pressure-style switch, there is no direct contact between the brake pedal arm and the switch. The switch instead is threaded into a brake line tee fitting that is installed within the brake line. As the brake pedal is depressed, an increase in brake fluid pressure is detected by the switch. A wire from each of the two electrical terminals on the end of the switch connect to the brake light circuit.

On this early 1960s Chevrolet, there are two taillights per side. Both are wired to serve as taillights, with one serving also as a brake light and the other also as a turn signal.

This steering column or turn-signal plug is used to connect wiring between the fuse panel and the steering column. Using a quick-disconnect plug allows the wires to be routed and connected one time, and then disconnected easily as required without fear of reconnecting wires incorrectly. These wires ultimately connect to the turn-signal lever on the steering column.

one time if necessary. Individual wires are then run from each turn-signal terminal on the fuse panel to the respective turn-signal light. Although color-coded wire is used to connect the turn signals (and most all automotive wiring as well), initially the multiple wires and possibility of faded colors makes using a plug a prudent practice to ensure correct operation.

Auxiliary Lighting: Most auxiliary lighting, such as foglights, driving lights, or special effect lighting, will include a schematic layout of how it should be connected electrically. Whether instructions are included or not, the auxiliary lighting will require power, ground, and a way to switch the lights ON or OFF. Since many of these auxiliary lights draw a significant amount of current, it is recommended to use a relay in addition to the light switch to prevent damage to the switch. (Refer to "Relays," page 62.) For that same reason, you may choose to run a separate ground wire from each light to a bolt on the engine block or to a ground stud to avoid problems caused by an ineffective ground.

Interior

On the inside of your vehicle, there are all sorts of lighting that may go unnoticed until it quits working for whatever

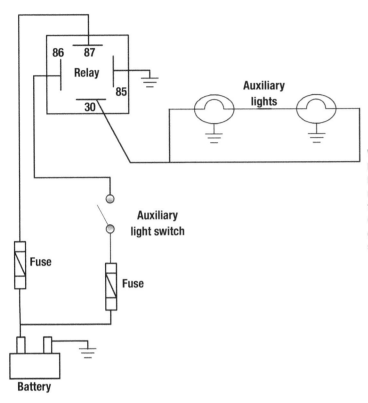

Whether they are foglights, driving lights, or something else, all auxiliary lighting systems will benefit if a relay is used, as most auxiliary lights require large amounts of current. Simply connect fused power to terminal 87 of the relay. Wire the switch for the auxiliary lights to another wire that connects to fused power on one end and to terminal 86 of the relay on the opposite end. Connect terminal 85 of the relay to a ground stud. Connect the power wire of the auxiliary lights to terminal 30 of the relay and connect the lights to a suitable ground.

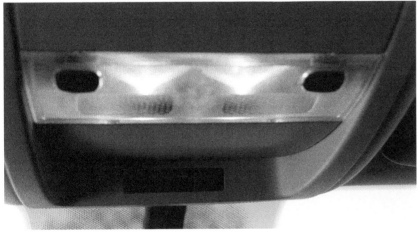

With a good understanding of electronics and all of the components available, it is easy to accessorize your vehicle as you please. This overhead map light comes ON when the door is opened and then fades out when the door is closed. Each side can also be turned ON or OFF manually by pressing the button (black spots) on the light you want to control.

reason. Most vehicles have a dome light and dash lights, while others may also have entry lights mounted in the doors, map or reading lights for each passenger, makeup lights mounted around a vanity mirror on the sun visor, cargo compartment lights, and underhood lamps. Although they are not lights, there are usually one if not several power outlets (formerly known as cigar lighters) to power a wide variety of accessories from cell phones to air compressors.

Courtesy: Courtesy lights in contemporary automobiles are available in a wide variety of configurations, sizes, and shapes. This makes salvage yards or even dealers' parts counters good

sources of interior lighting for use in a customized vehicle. Whether you are replacing one of these lights or installing one in a custom vehicle, the basics of a power source and a ground are the same. Some interior lights may have a manually operated switch at the light, while others will be wired to illuminate automatically.

How it works in your vehicle will depend on the light's internal switching mechanism and how you wire it in your vehicle. Some dome light circuits operate when ground is applied to the switch (commonly GM), while others (commonly Ford) operate when power is applied to the switch.

Flipping down the visor and opening the vanity mirror activates the lights, proving that most anything can be done with electricity.

The dome light in this 1968 Chevrolet pickup does not have a switch at the light, but can be turned ON or OFF by the driver by turning the headlight switch. Models with higher trim levels would have also included door-jamb switches that would activate the dome light when either door is opened.

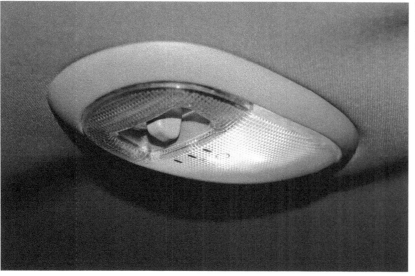

The dome light in this Chevrolet Equinox is wired so that it comes ON when the door is opened and then fades OFF. A three-way switch at the light allows for this automatic setting and also allows for a manual ON or a manual OFF position.

For common interior lighting that simply comes ON when a door is opened and goes OFF when the door is closed, door-jamb switches can be used. A door-jamb switch is designed so that when the door is closed, a plunger slides inward in the mounting, creating an open circuit (no dome light). When the door is opened, the plunger slides outward in the mounting, creating a closed circuit and thereby turning the courtesy lights ON.

Indicator: Common indicator lights are for high-beam headlights, turn signals, low engine oil pressure, high engine water temperature, door ajar, or even low windshield washer fluid level. This makes indicator lights slightly more complicated than courtesy lights, as the electrical circuit must include some sort of sensing switch (rather than a simple ON/OFF) that may be remotely located. The actual wiring of the sensing switch will vary from one vehicle manufacturer to another, so it is imperative to consult a wiring diagram specifically for the vehicle you are working on. For more on gauges and warning lights, refer to "Engine Monitoring Systems," page 64.

LED Lights

Light emitting diodes (LEDs) are becoming increasingly popular as automotive light sources, as they offer brighter light, are less likely to burn out, and require little power to operate when compared to filament bulbs. With these advantages come some disadvantages, but they are minimal when compared to the benefits of the LED lights. Still, their application requires some planning to be as effective.

LED lights are directional, so they are much brighter when viewed head on. This makes them great for use as a map light inside of the vehicle where you desire a bright light focused on a relatively small area. This directionality makes them somewhat unsuitable for use as a headlight, as that application requires light over a broad area.

The brightness of an LED light makes them superior for use as a taillight or brake light; however, their use requires

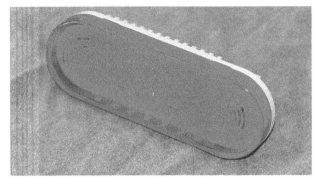

Each of the small circles in the lens of this LED utility light represents a light emitting diode, making this a very bright light when electric current is applied. If you use an LED light in a custom application, be sure to use a prismatic lens if the light is to be seen from anywhere besides directly in front of it.

a prismatic lens over the LED to disperse the light over a broader area. Without the dispersion characteristics of the prismatic lens, a brake light would not be easily seen from even a slight angle.

Additional Concerns: When using LEDs in turn-signal applications, extra attention must be used when selecting an appropriate flasher unit. For filament bulbs, a standard bi-metallic flasher that operates based on continuity (heat) switches the flashing lights ON and OFF repeatedly. The more lights that are on this type of circuit will create more heat, and therefore cause the lights to flash more rapidly. This type of flasher will not work properly with LED lights, as they do not create heat since they use less current.

When using LED lights in a turn-signal or hazard (flashing) situation, it will be necessary to use a no-load flasher to ensure that the lights flash properly. You must also keep this in mind when using LED turn signals in the rear of the vehicle and standard filament-type turn signals in the front. This situation may require two flashers to be wired into the circuit or to use a dummy load so that the LED portion of the circuit will flash.

These are a couple of indicator lights that could be used for a variety of uses. Commonly, they are used for turn signal or high-beam indicator lights. They could also be used to indicate that any circuit is open or closed as desired. Simply drill an appropriate size hole in the panel where you want the light mounted, push the light through from the front, connect one wire to a ground source, and then connect the other wire to the appropriate power wire.

Both of these flashers are for standard filament bulbs used as turn signals. The bulbs offer enough resistance to cause a bi-metallic strip to heat up and operate an internal timer that turns the signal lights ON and OFF repeatedly. LEDs do not heat up enough to cause this type of flasher to work properly. Both types of flashers look similar, however, so be sure to read the fine print when choosing your flasher.

TAILLIGHT AND BRAKE LIGHT PLACEMENT

While this book is intended to instruct on the proper wiring of automotive components rather than how to design a vehicle, I feel the need to at least briefly discuss effective placement of taillights and brake lights. This applies to both full-on custom vehicles and custom modifications to OEM vehicles. While most builders do not stray far from stock in headlight placement, they often choose to "clean up" the back of the vehicle by modifying the stock taillight arrangement. Perhaps this indicates that the original vehicle taillights were an afterthought by the designers; still, safety must be kept in the forefront of our conscience.

We must remember that taillight and brake light placement should be well within the normal line of sight of those driving behind us. If everyone drives with at least one car length for each 10 miles per hour of speed between them and the vehicle in front of them, this placement is not as important. When everyone is driving bumper to bumper and above the speed limit, however, brake lights need to be positioned strategically to be of any use. What this means is don't mount the taillights or brake lights too low on the vehicle. If the lights are too low on the vehicle in front of you, the front end of your vehicle will prevent you from seeing them. For this reason, a center high-mounted stop lamp (CHMSL), more commonly referred to as third brake light, has been mandated on all domestic vehicles manufactured since 1986.

While it will still be the fault of the person who runs into you if your vehicle gets crunched, do you really want that to happen just because you didn't like the look or placement of the taillights and brake lights on your vehicle? While a flashing billboard may be extreme, use some thought and good taste before you change the lighting on the back of your vehicle.

The stock taillights on this mid-1950s Ford station wagon are of good size (about 6 inches in diameter) and are mounted just a bit below the vehicle's beltline. As long as you are not following too closely, these lights would be easy enough to see.

While the Chevron taillight of the 1940 Ford is a classic, it is not the easiest to see. The chrome bezel is easy enough to see in the daylight, but the window area of the light itself is relatively small, especially in the slanted fender. Still, the 1940 Ford is thought by many to be one of the best-looking Fords ever built.

The taillights are smaller yet on this 1933–34 Ford coupe. While the light stands have been shortened and the lights therefore pulled closer to the fenders, the lights have not been altered from stock. The illuminated area is approximately 2 ½ inches in diameter but is not diminished by unnecessary decorative trim.

Somewhat decent-size taillights on this roadster are complemented by additional lights in the spreader bar. The spreader bar on the car is relatively low and the lights are small, however. This causes one to wonder how effectively this black car can be seen at night.

Okay, I really have to wonder about the effectiveness of this taillight, which is mounted vertically in the truck's fender. Can you find it? While I was able to find the taillight easily in person in the daylight, it was not much easier to see when illuminated. In case you cannot find the taillight, it is at the right side of the left light reflection. The orange paint of the truck was not removed from the light lens. Refer to the next photo for more details.

(continued on page 54)

TAILLIGHT AND BRAKE LIGHT PLACEMENT (continued from page 53)

This is a different truck but with the same type of taillights. These types of lights are designed to be mounted from the backside of the panel they are installed in, after an appropriately shaped and sized hole is cut in the panel. The panel and light lens is then sanded smooth. When the panel is painted, the paint is removed from the light lens during the color sanding process. Applications of clear do not adversely affect the light.

While it is not my desire or intent to berate other people's judgment, it seems that the two taillights mounted in the rear fenders would be too low for many other drivers to see. They are of good size, but only about a foot off the ground. The third brake light will help, but it is small and may be too high for many to see. Putting the third brake light between the rear window and the beltline would be more in line with other drivers' eyesight.

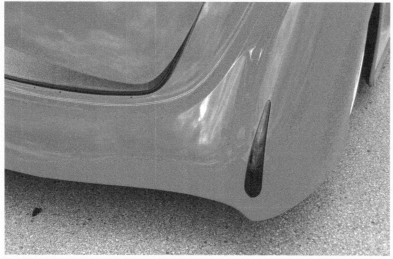

These taillights have more illuminated surface than what would have been stock and are blended into the vehicle very nicely, although they are a bit low on the car. While there may or may not be laws regarding what changes you can make to the taillights of your vehicle, you have to remember that they are there for a reason. I'm sure that you don't want your pride and joy getting crunched simply because you wanted your car to look cool.

Chapter 4
Switches

Switches are merely a method of controlling the flow of electricity. After all, with proper wiring, the electricity is already present. Switches allow us to turn an accessory ON, OFF, up, or down by closing or opening a circuit or by controlling how much voltage is allowed to reach that accessory.

Switches come in two types: those that are controlled manually and those that are controlled electromagnetically when voltage is applied across its coil. This latter type is known as a relay and has specific situations in which it should be used. After a discussion of various manually controlled switches, the uses for a relay will make more sense.

CHOOSING THE CORRECT SWITCH

Regardless of the type of switch, there are some concerns that must be addressed when choosing a switch. These are:

1. Will the switch fit in the desired location?
2. Can the switch carry the required amount of current?
3. Does the switch have enough internal circuits?
4. Does the switch have the required terminals?

If you are replacing or installing a new switch, you must choose a switch that will actually fit where you intend to put it, or find a different location. Quite often, the area behind the dash is filled with gauges, air conditioning and heater ducts, stereo equipment, and who knows what else from the outside. So before you replace a headlight switch or an ignition switch, you should check for available room before buying just any switch. You do not want any of these electrical components shorting out against each other.

To ensure a long service life of a switch, you must also verify that you do not overload it. Each switch should list the amount of volts and amperage that it is rated for. Exceeding these maximums is likely to cause problems that can and should be avoided.

The more jobs that a switch is required to do, the more internal circuits it must have. If a switch is to control just one operation, such as turning a fan ON or OFF, it requires just one circuit. A headlight switch that controls headlights, parking lights, and dome lights will require more internal circuits.

Any switch must also have enough terminals to enable you to connect the necessary wires to it. Ignition and headlight switches typically have the most wires connected to them. This is why a simple toggle switch is not used for

these applications on a street-legal vehicle. Vehicles that are not street legal usually do not have the various lighting and accessory options that require as many circuits.

TOGGLE SWITCHES

Toggle switches are very common and simple in that they are used to switch something ON or OFF. You were most likely aware of a toggle switch from a very early age when you learned to turn a light ON when you entered a dark room. Most residential room lights are controlled by a wall-mounted toggle switch near the doorway.

Both of these toggle switches are single-pole single-throw units, meaning they simply have two positions, ON and OFF. The unit on the left can handle one circuit, while the one on the right can handle multiple circuits.

Toggle switches are available in different configurations, sizes, and physical arrangement. Configurations commonly used in automotive wiring are single-pole single-throw, single-pole double-throw, and center-off. Knowing their differences and when to use them is important to using them correctly. Other than using a switch that is not capable of handling the electrical load, size of the switch is more of a styling or ergonomic preference. Physical arrangement simply refers to whether manual interface is done by flipping a lever, pushing a button, or any of a variety of other motions.

Single-Pole Single-Throw

A single-pole single-throw (SPST) switch can be thought of as a simple on-off switch. When the switch is closed (ON),

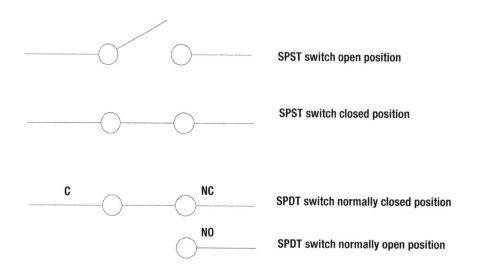

SPST switch open position

SPST switch closed position

C   NC   SPDT switch normally closed position

NO   SPDT switch normally open position

When an SPST switch is in the open position, the electrical circuit is open, so the accessory would be OFF. When an SPST switch is in the closed position, the electrical circuit is closed, so the accessory would be ON. When an SPDT switch is in the normally closed position, current is flowing to the accessory on that branch of the circuit, but not to the accessory on the normally open side. When an SPDT switch is in the normally open position, current is flowing to the accessory on that branch of the circuit but not to the accessory on the normally closed side.

electricity flows through the switch to power the accessory. When the switch is open (OFF), no electricity is flowing to the accessory. This type of switch will have only two electrical terminals, unless the switch itself includes a light, such as one that illuminates to indicate that the circuit is ON. In this case, the third electrical terminal is for a ground wire for the light.

Wiring this type of switch is easy because the wire providing power to the accessory to be controlled by the switch can be cut and the switch installed inline. In other words, the wire will begin at the power source, running to one terminal of the switch. Wire will then also connect to

the remaining terminal of the switch and run to the power electrical terminal of the accessory. Remember to ground the accessory to a suitable ground source.

Single-Pole Double- (or Dual-) Throw

Unlike a single-pole single-throw switch, a single-pole double-throw (SPDT) switch will be closed at all times, allowing electric current to flow to one of two terminals. This type of switch will have three terminals: a common, a normally closed, and a normally open. The wire from the power source connects to the common terminal. Wire also runs from the normally closed terminal to the accessory that will be used

This is another SPST toggle switch. Instead of a round toggle arm, this switch has a flat lever with a red handle. Other colors are also available, making color-coding an option for identifying various switches. This would typically be common in an offroad-oriented vehicle.

An SPDT switch is designed not to stop the flow of electricity completely, but rather to direct it from one path to another. One circuit that is connected to this type of switch will always be closed, while the other circuit will always be open, with the ability to switch circuits.

As a headlight dimmer switch, an SPDT is commonly used in automotive applications to switch between the main and an auxiliary fuel tank. The fuel will be pumped from one tank or the other at all times, unless, of course, that tank runs dry. You should switch tanks before running either tank completely dry, especially when using an electric fuel pump.

This is a replacement dimmer switch for a late model vehicle. When doing this type of repair, you should consult with a vehicle-specific service manual for both access and electrical connection info.

predominantly. Another wire runs from the normally open terminal to the secondary accessory. When power is applied, the position of the switch will dictate which accessory will be energized. If the switch is positioned to the normally closed position, the predominant accessory will be energized. If the switch is in the normally open position, the secondary accessory will be energized.

A common use for this type of switch is a headlight dimmer switch, which allows current to flow to the high-beam or the low-beam headlights, but not both at the same time. Another example of this type of switch in an automotive application is when two gas tanks are used in a vehicle. With the SPDT switch in one position, fuel will be used from one tank, but flipping the switch will cause fuel from the other tank to be used.

It is not really necessary to distinguish a circuit as predominant or secondary, as you may very well use each circuit the same amount of time. However, you must determine which circuit is which when you are doing the wiring.

Center Off

A common variation of the SPDT switch is the center-off switch. Like an SPDT, it has three electrical terminals, with two of them being normally open rather than one being normally closed. As the name implies, when the switch is in the center or neutral position, the circuit is open (no electric current is passing through the circuit). When the switch is moved to either one of the normally open positions, the accessory wired to the terminal is energized. The most common application of this type of switch is a turn-signal lever.

LIGHT SWITCHES

Except for various types of auxiliary lights (fog, driving, emergency), most lights within our automobiles are controlled by what is commonly referred to as the headlight switch. With vehicles that have courtesy lights, there is also a switch for each door. Typically, the headlight switch is either a push-pull type or a rotary type. That is, the lights are turned ON by pulling the knob out and turned OFF by pushing the knob in or are controlled based on the position of a rotary dial.

Headlight Switch

Regardless of the type of headlight switch you have, they are typically wired in the same way. The portion of the headlight switch that is mounted behind the dash panel will have

This is an extremely simple headlight switch, or more appropriately a push-pull switch. Pulling the knob out closes the circuit, while pushing the knob in opens the circuit. There are only two terminals (power in and power out), so use as a headlight switch would require that relays be used to control dome lights or parking lights, if used.

The headlight switch on my 2008 Chevy Silverado is a rotary. The "auto" setting turns the daytime running lamps ON when the vehicle is running and turns the headlights and taillights ON when ambient light drops below a predetermined level. This setting also turns all of the lights OFF when the vehicle is not running. The next setting clockwise turns ON only the parking lights, front and rear. Turning the knob fully clockwise manually turns the headlights and taillights ON.

multiple electrical terminals to which a number of wires are connected. At the minimum, there will be three electrical terminals: power to the switch, power to the high-beam circuit, and power to the low-beam circuit. In more complex automobiles, there will also be electrical terminals for dash instrument lights, parking lights, daytime running lights, dome and courtesy lights, and possibly others, depending on the vehicle.

The actual connection of wiring to the switch will vary by manufacturer but will usually become obvious when you actually gain access to the switch. Some will use ring connectors, while others will use push-on terminal connectors. What will potentially be difficult is knowing which wire to connect to which terminal, as some switches are labeled, but others are not. To find out which terminal does what, you will need to use a continuity tester or at minimum a test light. With a power source connected to the switch and the continuity tester or test light connected to a suitable ground, probe each electrical terminal while the switch is in each of its various positions.

Of course, it will help if you have a wiring schematic for your vehicle, but the following will provide a place to start if a wiring schematic is not available. The switch position for headlights ON is typically when the switch knob is pulled

The plunger shown at the right end of this door jamb switch is spring loaded and is operated by the closed door pushing against it. Wiring connections take place on the opposite end. When the plunger is out (as shown) the circuit closes and turns the courtesy lights ON. When the door closes, the plunger pushes inward causing the circuit to open, turning the courtesy lights OFF.

fully out or turned fully to the right, with OFF being the opposite. Daytime running lights or parking lights ON is somewhere in between. You will need to take some notes while you are probing each terminal to accurately determine the correct terminals. When the switch is in position for the parking lights only to be ON, there will be current at the terminal for the parking lights, but not at the headlight power terminal. When the headlight switch is in position for the headlights to be ON, there will be current at the headlight terminal and the terminal for the parking lights. At the headlight switch, there will typically be just one terminal for the headlight power. A wire from this terminal should be routed to the dimmer switch. At that point, headlight power is divided into two circuits: high-beam and low-beam.

Some headlight switches will include a rheostat. This is used to manually dim or brighten the dash and instrument lights and the courtesy lights. Just to clarify, this rheostat has nothing to do with the dimmer switch that is used to switch between high-beam and low-beam headlights.

Door-Jamb Switch

You have no doubt noticed that in most vehicles, a dome light and possibly courtesy lights located in the door usually come on when you or a passenger open one of the doors. This is made possible by having a door jamb switch located inline with the interior lights at each door. Wiring will vary between switches, but the intent is for the switch to be open while the door is pushing against it so that the light is OFF. When the door is opened, the switch changes positions, the circuit closes, and the light comes ON. While the plunger being pushed in by the door is what activates the switch, you must be careful to wire the door jamb switch correctly. Some switches are designed to illuminate their respective lights upon application of ground, while other switches are designed to illuminate upon application of power.

A variation of the push-button–style door-jamb switch is a magnetic door-jamb switch. This style uses a magnet and a reed switch to turn the dome lights ON or OFF. Typically, a magnet is mounted into the opening edge of the door. A reed switch is mounted in the stationary portion of the body (door post). Design of a reed switch allows the contacts to be normally open (closing when a magnetic field is present) or normally closed (opening when the magnetic field is present). For this reason, the wiring must be correct, otherwise the dome light will be ON when the door is closed and OFF when the door is opened.

While they are not exactly switches, now is a good time to mention wireless connectors since they are used in door jambs. Wireless connectors are made up of spring-loaded rounded solid brass contacts that can slide within a housing that is mounted in the door jamb. A similar connector is mounted in the door so that the connectors will align. When the door is closed, the brass contacts in the door and the door jamb make contact, closing the circuit. When the door is open, the brass contacts no longer make contact, opening the circuit. These types of contacts are often used for power windows, power door locks, or stereo speakers.

DIMMER SWITCHES

One power wire from the headlights terminal of the headlight switch connects to the dimmer switch. There are then two wires exiting the opposite side of the switch. One serves as power to the high-beam light circuit, while the other serves as power to the low-beam light circuit. As we know from earlier reading in this chapter, a dimmer switch is a single-pole double-throw switch. Either the high-beam lights or the low-beam lights can be on, but not both at the same time. If your vehicle uses a four-light headlamp system, however, it is quite possible to wire the lights so that all four will be ON when the high-beam lights are ON. In fact, in older vehicles, four headlight systems were wired so that all four lights were ON when the high beams were ON.

While it is not mandatory, there are two distinct advantages of installing a relay between the headlight switch and the dimmer switch. Since the headlights are a heavy current accessory, using a relay will allow the headlight switch to last longer. Additionally, the headlights will burn brighter.

Dimmer switches were commonly mounted on the floor in vehicles manufactured in the 1960s and earlier but were transitioned to being positioned on the left side of the steering column after that time. Perhaps this is the reason that no one uses turn signals anymore. No one realizes that the lever on the left side of the steering column has multiple uses.

If a floor-mounted dimmer switch must be replaced, it can usually be done by unplugging the dimmer switch wiring from the dimmer switch and then removing one or two bolts that secure the dimmer switch to the vehicle's floor. The new dimmer switch can then be secured to the floor and the wiring plugged into it.

Removing or replacing a column-mounted dimmer switch is slightly more tricky. You will no doubt need to remove at least one or two panels from around the steering column and quite possibly remove the steering wheel itself. These are not difficult tasks to accomplish, but they will vary somewhat from one vehicle to another. If your vehicle uses a column-mounted dimmer switch, you should consult a vehicle-specific repair manual prior to service. The last thing you want to do while repairing a dimmer switch is to activate an air bag.

This floor-mounted switch is a common example of a single pole double throw (SPDT) switch. The headlight power wire from the headlight switch connects to the single terminal going into the switch. A power wire to the high-beam circuit and another power wire to the low-beam circuit attach each connect to one of the two terminals coming out of the switch. Switching is manually activated by pushing the cap.

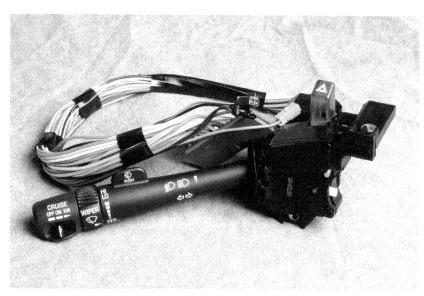

A column-mounted dimmer switch is much more complicated than a floor-mounted unit, as the same assembly in this case controls the cruise control, wiper delay, windshield washer pump, turn signals, and high and low beams of the headlights. In this example, there are two separate plugs that simply plug into the existing wiring harness, making the electrical connections the simplest portion of the reinstallation process.

IGNITION SWITCHES

An ignition switch is similar to a headlight switch in that different positions of the switch allow for current to flow through different electrical circuits. A major difference in the two is that an ignition switch includes two distinct parts: one is the lock cylinder that the key is inserted into, while the second is the actual electrical switch mechanism. Difficulty with either one will cause distinct problems, but most likely will call for replacement of the ignition switch in either case.

If the tumblers in the lock become stripped, the key may fall out of the ignition, the lock cylinder may not turn, or possibly any key could be used to start the ignition. If the electrical switch is faulty, it may become impossible to start the engine.

Replacement of the ignition switch is not difficult, especially in an older vehicle where the ignition switch is typically mounted in the dash. On newer vehicles where the ignition switch is located in the steering column, replacement is more complicated due mostly to anti-theft devices within the steering column and the ignition switch. When servicing an ignition switch, you must disconnect both battery cables (both negative *and* positive) from the battery or shut off a master disconnect switch before service begins, as live wires would otherwise be present.

Dash-Mounted

Depending on the vehicle, a dash-mounted ignition switch may be able to be removed by simply unthreading a collar

This universal dash-mounted ignition switch is designed for connections to be made with ring terminals. Connecting circuits to the "accessory" stud allows for accessories to be powered and operational when just the accessory circuit is ON. Connecting circuits to the "run" stud powers them only while the engine is running.

This is the lock cylinder portion of a column-mounted ignition switch. When the key is turned, the knob on the opposite end of the cylinder rotates within an opening in the electrical switch mechanism, causing the electrical contacts to align.

from the front side of the switch and then pulling the switch through to the back side of the dash. Prior to disconnecting the wires from the terminals, you should mark or tag each of the wires so that they can be reconnected correctly. The new switch is then installed by reconnecting the wires, pushing the switch through the dash panel and then securing it in place with the threaded collar. You must verify that the outer housing of the switch cannot turn in the dash panel, or you will not be able to turn the key within the switch to start the engine.

Some vehicles with dash-mounted ignition switches have different methods of securing the switch within the dash panel. So it may be necessary to consult a vehicle-specific repair manual for instructions on how to remove the switch mechanism. After removing the switch, however, the wiring process will be similar to most other dash-mounted ignition switches.

Column-Mounted

Removing or replacing a steering column–mounted ignition switch will present similar obstacles as servicing a steering column–mounted dimmer switch. One or two panels will need to be removed from around the steering column, as well as the steering wheel itself on some models. These are not difficult tasks to accomplish, but they will vary somewhat from one vehicle to another. If your vehicle utilizes a column mounted ignition switch, you should consult a vehicle specific repair manual prior to service. Be sure that you do not damage or deploy the air bag.

RELAYS

While electrical relays tend to confuse those unfamiliar with them, they are really nothing more than an electromagnetic switch. Simply put, a relay is a low-current device to control a high-current accessory. A typical switch is operated manually, while a relay switches when voltage is applied.

Relays are used for three basic reasons: reliability, serviceability, and to use a low-current controller to operate a high-current device. If the circuit will have current in excess of 10 amps, a relay will prove to be more reliable than a standard switch. Multiple relays for multiple circuits can be centrally located, making troubleshooting and diagnostic efforts easier. Typical relays also require little current to operate, which makes them more compatible with many of the switches and controllers used in modern automobiles. It is common to use a relay to switch headlights, foglights, a hydraulic brake light switch, or an electric fan, but many other uses exist.

The relay is made up of two distinct parts: the switch and the coil that causes the switch to be thrown when power is applied. Like regular switches, relays can be of the SPST (single-pole single-throw) or SPDT (single-pole double-throw) variety, so you must pay particular attention

to the relay to verify that you are using the correct type for the application.

Most relays have a number near each terminal and a wiring schematic printed on the side. An SPST relay will have terminals labeled 85, 86, 30, and 87. A SPDT relay will have those same terminals but will also include a terminal marked 87a.

To provide a practical example of how to actually wire a relay, consider an electric fan. A terminal on the fuse block will have two wires running from it. One of those will connect to terminal 85 to provide 12 volts of power to the relay's coil. Somewhere in this wire, a switch will need to be installed, so that you can manually turn the fan ON or OFF. An inline fuse for two or three amps can be installed to protect the switch. The second of these power wires will connect to terminal 30, which is the common terminal in the relay. This wire should be fused (at the fuse panel) for the load of the fan (or whatever accessory that you are using the relay on). A third wire will connect terminal 86 on the relay to a suitable ground. The fourth wire will connect terminal 87 of the relay to the power side of the fan. Note that the fan will also require its own ground wire.

When purchasing a relay, verify that it is of the same type as the one you are replacing. If you were to replace an SPDT relay mistakenly with an SPST, it simply will not work correctly. Also, you must size the relay for the load on the circuit, such as 30 amps or 40 amps. This is not the amount of current that is required to operate the relay, but rather the amount of current that the relay can adequately handle. As with switches and wire, go with a larger rating than what is actually required.

Relay	Terminal Connection
85*	Coil input (+12VDC)
86*	Coil input (to ground)
30	Common
87	Normally open
87a	Normally closed

* Terminals 85 and 86 can be interchanged.

SOLENOID SWITCHES

Solenoid switches are used in most automotive starter systems but can also be used for other types of switching mechanisms. A solenoid itself is composed of a loop of wire (also called a coil) wrapped around a metallic core (see Figures on page 12). When electric current is introduced to the coil, a magnetic field is created. This metallic core is known as the armature or plunger. There is also a stop that limits the movement of the armature. Depending on the polarity of the coil, the stop will become a north or south pole, while the armature becomes a south or north pole. These opposite poles attract, allowing movement of the armature, based on the absence or presence of electrical current.

Starter Solenoid

When you turn the key in the ignition switch, it sends a small amount of electric current to the starter solenoid. This in turn causes a pair of electric contacts to close, which then closes the electric circuit to the starter motor. When all is good, the engine then starts. If, however, an insufficient amount of electric current reaches the starter solenoid, the contacts that close the circuit for the starter motor will remain open and the starter motor never spins. When this happens, you typically hear a clicking noise. This means that the starter solenoid is getting some power, but not enough to spin the starter motor. Common causes are corroded or loose connections at the battery or starter solenoid, a bad positive cable from the battery, or a low or dead battery.

Door Latch and Lock Solenoid

Solenoid switches can also be used to lock or unlock doors and open or close windows. These types of switches have been used for several decades among the custom-car crowd. By having a magnet located in a specific location in the vehicle, the owner of a custom "lead sled" could rub that same area of the car with another magnet to open the car doors. The downside of this technology was that it would eventually wear the lacquer paint off the magnet's location, making it easy for others with similar magnetic "keys" to gain access. Contemporary vehicles with keyless entry systems use the same basic technology but operate it with radio signals that are much easier on the vehicle's finish.

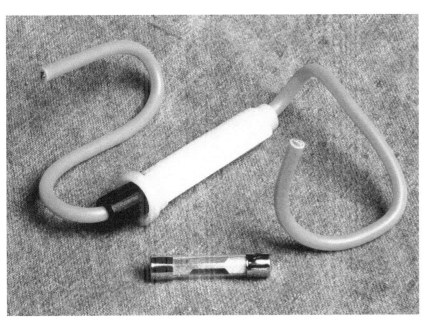

Anytime that you are powering an accessory through a relay, the wire powering the relay should be fused. This can be done easily by installing an inline fuse holder and then installing the correct size fuse for the application. Simply strip approximately 3/8 inch of the insulation from each end of the inline fuse holder and a similar amount from each wire that it is to be connected to. Then use butt connectors to install the inline fuse holder.

Chapter 5
Engine-Monitoring Systems

Engine-monitoring systems simply refer to the dash panel gauges that keep us aware of what is going on under the hood of our automobiles. It can also refer to the warning lights that illuminate to tell us that we were not paying close enough attention and that there is a problem. Regardless of how much information is monitored or presented to the driver, it is the driver's responsibility to understand that information and act accordingly.

AMMETER AND VOLTMETER

Either of these provide information about the electrical system, with ammeters generally being used with generators, while voltmeters are generally used with alternators. An ammeter is designed to measure current flow to or from the battery. Under normal conditions, this flow will be to the battery. If the generator or alternator system fails, however, the ammeter will measure discharge flow from the battery. So, if you are recharging a low battery, an ammeter will indicate a higher value. Likewise, if the battery is fully charged, the voltage regulator reduces flow, causing the ammeter to indicate a lower flow rate. In an ideal situation, the ammeter would be reading zero.

Since an ammeter is measuring flow (amps), all of those amps must be routed through the ammeter to obtain an accurate reading. This requires that the ammeter itself be able to withstand this amount of amperage flowing through it. Additionally, a heavy-gauge wire must be routed from the electrical system to carry this flow to the ammeter, which could cause a fire hazard if the wire is not sized adequately. If the gauge should fail, you would lose all power from your alternator or generator.

Instead of a flow meter, a voltmeter measures pressure in volts. When an alternator and its voltage regulator are working correctly to keep the battery charged, the voltmeter should read between 14.0 and 14.5 volts. If the alternator system fails, the voltage in the battery will begin to drop and will be reflected by the reading of the voltmeter.

Since all of the voltage is not required to flow through the voltmeter, installation of a voltmeter is quicker, safer, and easier. All that is necessary is a 14-gauge wire connected to a fused, ignition-switched source. Most aftermarket wiring kits will indicate a specific wire from the fuse panel that is to be connected to the voltmeter.

An ammeter provides an indication of which way electric current is flowing in relationship to the battery. If the battery is charging, the number of amperes would be positive, while they would be negative if the battery is discharging. In a perfect electrical system, the ammeter would be reading at zero.

A voltmeter measures pressure in volts, enabling it to determine how much voltage is available in the electrical system at any one time. Unlike other gauges that will require electric power and some type of sender input, electric power through a fused, ignition-switched source serves as both.

FUEL LEVEL

A fuel-level gauge does not indicate how many gallons of fuel are left in the tank, but it merely approximates how much of the tank's overall capacity is still available, such as three-quarters, half, or a quarter tank. The fuel-level gauge has two distinct components: the fuel-level sending unit and the gauge itself.

This aftermarket fuel-level gauge is marked in one-eighth increments. The accuracy, however, depends largely on how accurately the fuel-level sender is calibrated. If, for instance, the sender is calibrated for a tank that is 15 inches deep but the tank is only 10 inches deep, you may run out of gas without warning. Conversely, if the sender were calibrated for a 10-inch deep tank, but the tank were actually 15 inches deep, you could drive farther even though the gauge indicates that it's empty.

The fuel-level sending unit includes a float, an arm, and a variable resistor, all of which are connected to a bracket that is inserted through an opening in the top of the tank. The float (that floats at the top of the fuel) is attached to one end of an arm that also connects to a variable resistor that is actually connected to the mounting bracket. As the float rides up or down with the level of the fuel, it moves a wiper along a strip of bimetallic metal that is grounded on one end. When the float moves so that the wiper is closer to the grounded end of the bimetallic strip, there is less resistance, and when the float moves so that the wiper is farther away from the grounded end, there is more resistance. This amount of resistance (small or large) is what causes the fuel-level gauge to operate. The gauge and sender must be compatible (the sender must operate on the correct ohm values) for proper operation.

Some gauges are designed so that a small amount of resistance indicates a full tank and a large amount indicates an empty tank, while other gauges are designed just the opposite. Regardless, when purchased new, the gauge and sender will come with installation instructions and specific readings for full and empty so that you can be sure to install the gauge and sending unit properly.

Some things to remember when installing a new fuel-level gauge are grounding and calibration. The fuel-level gauge and the sender will each need to be grounded. If your fuel-level gauge begins operating erratically, that is a good sign that it has a faulty ground. Additionally, the arm length must be adjusted during installation to compensate for the depth of the tank. While it is always a good idea to disconnect the negative battery cable from the battery when doing any

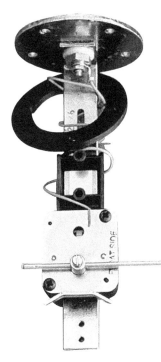

The float (white ball in this photo) at the end of an arm activates a variable resistor as it travels up and down with the fuel level in the tank. At the time of installation, the float must be located a specified distance from its pivot point to correspond with the depth of the tank. Likewise, the variable resistor must be located on the mounting bracket at a specific location as indicated on the instructions.

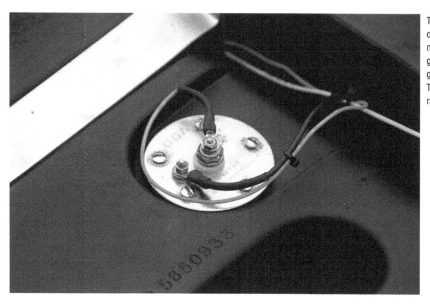

The fuel-level sender is secured to the tank by a number of screws (typically five or six), depending on the manufacturer. The red wire in the photo runs to the fuel gauge mounted in the dash panel. The black wire runs to a ground stud mounted on the vehicle's rear crossmember. The yellow wire comes from a relay mounted to the frame rail and provides power to the fuel pump.

wiring, it is especially important to do so and eliminate any sparks when working with the fuel-level sender or an electric fuel pump since gasoline vapors may be present.

OIL PRESSURE

An electrical oil-pressure gauge simply reads an electrical voltage output from an oil-pressure sensor that is threaded into the engine block. This electric-voltage output is in direct proportion to the oil pressure. When the engine is not running, the oil-pressure gauge should read 0 but should rise immediately when you start the engine.

If you suspect the oil-pressure gauge of being faulty, disconnect the wire from the sending unit, ground that wire, and turn the ignition key ON. The oil-pressure gauge should immediately read at its highest reading if the gauge is working properly. If the gauge does not immediately read at the highest point, the oil-pressure sending unit is faulty and should be replaced. Whenever replacing an oil-pressure sending unit, wrap the threads of the sending unit with Teflon tape prior to installation.

A note about Teflon tape and/or liquid sealant and sending units: There seems to be a pretty even split in opinions

An oil-pressure gauge shows the pressure of the lubricating oil within the engine block. When the engine is not running, the pressure within the block and the reading on the gauge should read 0. When the engine is idling, the pressure will typically drop somewhat from the vehicle's "normal" reading.

Wrap the threads of the oil-pressure sending unit with Teflon tape, and then thread the sender into an oil galley in the engine block. It may be necessary to use an angle adaptor between the engine block and oil-pressure sending unit to gain enough clearance. After the sending unit is installed, connect the sensor wire to the top of the sending unit with a ring terminal secured by a nut, and then connect the opposite end of the wire to the oil-pressure gauge.

between using and not using Teflon tape on the threads of oil pressure and water temperature gauge senders. Without the tape, you risk the leakage of engine oil or engine coolant, respectively. With the tape, you risk the tape becoming an insulator and not having an adequate electrical ground at the sender. I would suggest installing the senders first without Teflon, and then check for leakage on a regular basis for a while. If the gauges work properly and there is no leakage, all is good. If there is some leakage, remove the sender, apply Teflon, and reinstall the sender. Check for proper operation of the gauges and for leakage. Personally, I used Teflon on the sending units in the '68 Chevy C10 that was rewired as part of this book and have no problems with the gauges grounding.

WATER TEMPERATURE

The water-temperature gauge simply reads the temperature of the coolant that is flowing through the engine block and radiator. Since this temperature will vary, depending on where it is measured, the most accurate location for a water-temperature sensor to be placed is in the cylinder head since that is where the temperature is most critical. The sensor threads should be wrapped with Teflon tape prior to installation to prevent leakage of coolant. You should also use a wrench to tighten the sensor in the cylinder head. Water temperature is relayed to the temperature gauge through a wire. Like all other gauges, the water-temperature gauge must be grounded to work properly.

A water-temperature gauge indicates the temperature of the coolant (antifreeze and water) flowing through the engine. This is merely the temperature at the location of the sending unit; however, deviations from "normal" for your particular vehicle should be cause for concern. For most accurate temperature readings, the sending unit should be placed in the cylinder head.

Wrap the threads of the water-temperature sending unit with Teflon tape, and then thread the sender into a water jacket in the engine block. If the hole in the engine block and the sending unit are not the same size, it will be necessary to use an adaptor between the two. After the sending unit is installed, connect the sensor wire to the top of the sending unit with an appropriate connection and then connect the opposite end of the wire to the water-temperature gauge.

ENGINE-MONITORING SYSTEMS

SPEEDOMETER

The speedometer provides the driver with the speed of the vehicle, and, depending on the make and model of the vehicle, will display in MPH (miles per hour), Km/H (kilometers per hour), or both. Although exact wiring of speedometers will vary from one manufacturer to the next, they will be somewhat similar. Each speedometer will require a connection to a fused power source, a suitable ground, and input directly or indirectly from the transmission. The input from the transmission may be through a Hall-effect sensor, an inductive sensor, or an electronic control box.

Many aftermarket gauge kits offer mechanical or electrical speedometers, even if the rest of the gauges in the kit are electric. A benefit of an electric speedometer is that it can be easily programmed by the driver. While this may not be of interest to anyone with an ordinary daily driver vehicle, it is of great benefit if you ever change tire sizes or rear-end gears. You would simply go through a relatively simple recalibration process, rather than be required to change the drive gear that is typically located in the transmission for a mechanical speedometer.

Calibration of a programmable speedometer will vary from manufacturer, but the simplest procedure is to drive the vehicle in question to a stretch of highway that has an exact 1-mile distance marked. You can either measure this 5,280-foot distance yourself (not likely!) or use the mile markers often found along the highway. You would then go through a preliminary set of instructions to begin the calibration, and then drive the exact 1-mile distance, stop, and then follow some ending instructions. This process would then calibrate the speedometer and therefore the odometer. You can also adjust the speedometer with the vehicle on a dynamometer.

The speedometer shows the vehicle's speed and in this case is in 2-mile-per-hour increments. The window near the lower middle of the gauge is the odometer and shows the total number of miles the vehicle has been driven. Neither speed nor distance is registered until the speedometer is calibrated. Since this is a new installation, speedometer calibration is still on the list of tasks to finish.

Most aftermarket electric speedometers include a plug and connectors similar to these so that all wires connecting to the back of the speedometer can be plugged or unplugged as one connection to prevent mismatching wires and terminals. If a plug is not available, each connection can be made separately, but should be labeled if disconnected, to aid in reassembly.

TACHOMETER

A tachometer (also called a tach) indicates the revolutions per minute (rpm) the engine is turning. This is especially useful in racing so that the driver can manually shift the transmission at the best time to take advantage of the vehicle's engine rpm. Many contemporary automobiles include a tach as standard equipment, even though they have an automatic transmission. Other than as a diagnostic tool, I personally don't understand having a tach in a vehicle with an automatic transmission, even though I did install one in my '68 Chevy pickup that is wired later in this book.

Just like the speedometer discussed previously, wiring for a tachometer will vary by manufacturer. However, the tach will require a connection to a fused power source, a suitable ground, and input from an electronic-ignition control box, the ignition coil, or from the tach signal from the alternator. With all gauges, consult the installation instructions provided with the gauges for more detailed information.

A tachometer indicates how fast the engine is turning. Knowing this is especially useful so the driver knows when to shift gears, whether in a manual or automatic transmission–equipped vehicle. When used with an automatic transmission, this is pertinent information if pulling a trailer. In addition, some drivers simply want to keep track of how hard their engine is working (and consuming fuel) at various cruising speeds. All tachometers will indicate a factor (rpm x 100 in this case) that the reading should be multiplied by for the correct reading. In this example, if the needle was on "20," the engine would be running at 2,000 rpm.

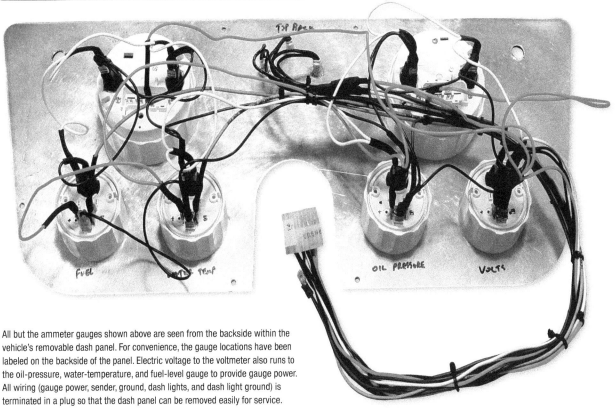

All but the ammeter gauges shown above are seen from the backside within the vehicle's removable dash panel. For convenience, the gauge locations have been labeled on the backside of the panel. Electric voltage to the voltmeter also runs to the oil-pressure, water-temperature, and fuel-level gauge to provide gauge power. All wiring (gauge power, sender, ground, dash lights, and dash light ground) is terminated in a plug so that the dash panel can be removed easily for service.

ELECTRONIC-CONTROL MODULE AND ELECTRONIC-CONTROL UNIT

The electronic-control module (ECM), electronic-control unit (ECU), and central-control module (CCM) are all generic terms for what we typically refer to as a vehicle's computer. It should perhaps be referred to as a computer network, as there are several ECMs, ECUs, and CCMs in any contemporary motor vehicle. Regardless of what we call it, this collection of computers controls some or all of the electrical systems within the vehicle. While there are many more, some of the more common electronic-control units are the airbag-control unit (ACU); body-control module (BCM) that controls power door locks, windows, and courtesy lights; onboard diagnostics (OBD); powertrain-control module (PCM); and transmission-control unit (TCU).

Each of these electronic-control modules receives data from sensors located throughout the system being monitored. Some of the more common ones are oxygen sensor, coolant sensor, mass-airflow sensor, air-intake sensor, throttle-position sensor, and knock sensor. Whenever information from any of these sensors is outside of their parameters, the electronic-control module stores a diagnostic trouble code and illuminates a malfunction indicator lamp (MIL) more commonly known as the "check engine light." To determine the malfunction, you or a repairman will be required to use an OBD diagnostic tool that plugs into a port located somewhere beneath or near the dash.

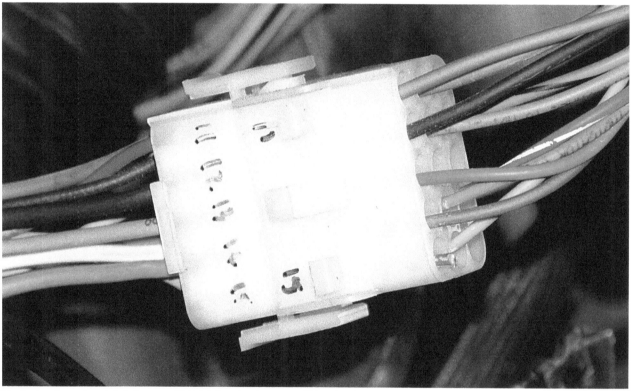

The plug from the previous photo (bottom, page 69) fits into its mate only one way; still, I numbered each terminal to verify that I installed each wire in the correct location. The plug's mate was numbered in the same fashion. Additionally, terminal numbers and wire color for each half of the connection were recorded on a piece of paper for easy reference.

Chapter 6
Accessories Circuits

In addition to the normal ignition and lighting circuits, there are various other electrical circuits that are commonly part of a vehicle modification or customization. It is not necessary to completely rewire a vehicle to include these circuits, but knowing how to add them correctly is critical. Most often, knowing to use a relay to control the accessory's operation will save you lots of trouble later.

Many contemporary overdrive transmissions are operated electronically, so if they are not wired correctly, they simply will not work correctly. Electric fuel pumps are easier to install than a mechanical fuel pump and can also offer more fuel delivery, which may be a necessity in high-performance applications. While driving a hot rod is cool in itself, there is no reason to not be comfortable, so an HVAC system makes good sense. If you have a big engine in a little car, an electric cooling fan may be the best way to keep the engine from overheating. Power windows, doors, and seats are common upgrades for most any kind of vehicle. Unless you are completely rewiring your vehicle, it may simply be easier to add an auxiliary fuse panel to provide power for these accessories, rather than attempt to tie into an already overloaded fuse panel.

Do not forget to provide easy access to electrical components that may someday require programming or other service. While it is easy enough to run the wiring and then cover it up, it may be necessary to reprogram an engine that is equipped with electronic fuel injection. If an electric fuel pump is located inside the fuel tank, remember to allow for access so that you are not required to remove the fuel tank to service the fuel pump.

This is the electric fuel pump used in the rewiring of the '68 Chevy pickup later in this book. When installing an electric fuel pump, mount the pump as low as possible in relation to the tank. Also verify that fuel lines in and out of the pump correspond to the flow indicator markings on the pump itself. Since a fuel pump is a high-current accessory, do yourself a favor and install a relay within the pump's wiring.

TRANSMISSION LOCKUP

Many automatic transmission torque converters now include a lockup clutch, which improves the efficiency of the transmission and reduces heat caused by torque convert slippage. When the clutch locks, the torque converter's turbine and pump become mechanically locked together, eliminating the fluid flow interference and turbulence-related inefficiencies. In transmissions that have this feature, the clutch typically locks at highway cruising speeds, so it effectively works as an overdrive to increase gas mileage. This mechanical coupling takes place through a lockup solenoid. The lockup solenoid valve is controlled by the vehicle's computer. For more information on servicing the transmission lockup solenoid on your vehicle, refer to a model-specific repair manual.

ELECTRIC FUEL PUMPS

Electric fuel pumps electrically require only power and ground, so installation is straightforward; however, most electric fuel pumps draw a large amount of current, so it is good practice to install a relay in the fuel pump circuit. As we already know about relays, they are easy to install and provide maintenance-free operation of high-current electric components.

To install an electric fuel pump, first mount the gas tank if not done already. Some electric fuel pumps actually mount in the fuel tank, while others mount outside of the tank. Electric fuel pumps work more effectively at pushing fuel, rather than siphoning fuel. So if the pump is to be mounted outside of the tank, it should be mounted relatively close to and lower than the tank. Fuel line should then be routed from the tank to the inlet side of the fuel pump and from the outlet side of the fuel pump to the engine's induction system.

The fuel pump relay (SPST) can be mounted wherever is convenient. If it is mounted near other relays, it should be labeled by application (e.g., fuel pump) for future troubleshooting or servicing purposes. Connect a 12-gauge wire from the fuel pump terminal on the fuse panel to provide 12 VDC to terminals 85 and 30 of the relay. You can do this by running two separate wires from the fuse panel, or more efficiently by running one wire from the fuse panel to the terminal 86 and then using a jumper wire between terminals 86 and 87. If running two wires, each should have a 10-amp inline fuse. If just one of these wires goes back to the fuse panel, then one 10-amp inline fuse will be required. Connect a ground wire to terminal 85 and to a suitable ground. Power to the fuel pump will be completed by running a wire from terminal 30 to the power side of the fuel pump and a ground wire from the ground side of the fuel pump to a suitable ground. When working with relays, remember that the relay does not care which way the electricity is flowing, so terminals 86 and 85 can be interchanged with each other and terminals 87 and 30 can be interchanged with each other.

HVAC SYSTEM (A/C, HEAT, AND DEFROST)

Providing cool air, warm air, and defrost to your vehicle is all done by the same system. How the air is cooled or heated is beyond the scope of this book; however, electrical wiring does play a part in controlling, directing, and moving that air. Other than the actual control panel that the operator uses, most operation of the HVAC (heating, ventilation, and air conditioning) is internally controlled by one or multiple relays, depending on the sophistication of the system.

At the risk of oversimplifying the process, in a typical system, power is provided to a power relay from the fuse panel. Switched power is also connected to the power relay so that the HVAC system can be operated only when the vehicle is running. The power relay must also be grounded. Finally, this power relay connects to the fan switch located on the control panel and to a fan relay. A connection to the control panel also serves to provide switched power to the fan relay that ultimately provides power to the blower motor.

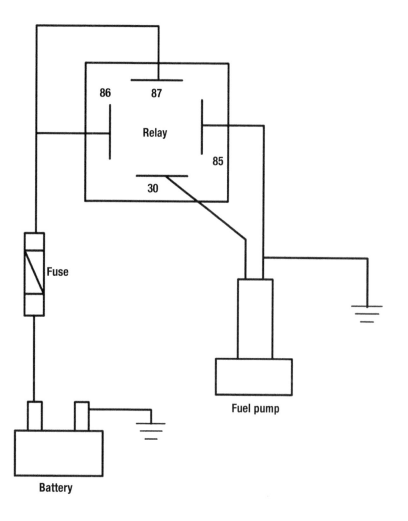

Electric fuel pumps draw a lot of current and when they go bad will leave you stranded along the side of the road without the least bit of remorse. To minimize the potential of being stranded due to a bad fuel pump, install it with an SPST relay.

The control panel also directly or indirectly connects to an air-conditioning microswitch, a heater microswitch, and a defrost microswitch. These all control the doors within the duct system to direct the air to the correct air ducts. An air-conditioning thermostat connects to a compressor safety switch and then to a compressor clutch. This is what controls the compressor. The air-conditioning thermostat also connects to both the air-conditioning and defrost microswitches. A heater valve vacuum solenoid connects to the heater microswitch. All relays, the blower motor, and the heater valve vacuum solenoid must be grounded.

Whether you are servicing an existing air-conditioning system in your vehicle or installing a new system, most of the wiring should already be intact. Other than replacing damaged wire, faulty connections, or a failed relay, most of the wiring within the system should be left as is. Still, you will need to provide power and ground to the system. Consult a vehicle-specific service manual for service on an existing system or the installation manual for the specific air-conditioning system you are installing for specific instructions.

ELECTRIC FANS

There are multiple reasons for installing an electric cooling fan (as opposed to a mechanical cooling fan), but the most important reason for either electric or mechanical is to cool the engine. To do that, a shroud should be used to force air to flow over the entire radiator. In addition to that, the fan should be capable of moving at least 2,500 cubic feet per minute (cfm) to make it worth your while. From an electrical perspective, three components are required for successful installation and proper operation. Those are a fuse, a thermostat, and a relay.

A fuse should be installed inline between the fuse panel and the relay and be rated at no more than 3 amps. It is important to include this fuse, as it is the last line of safety should your electric fan develop an electrical problem. A thermostat should be wired inline into the system to control the fan (turn it ON and OFF). You could simply install a manually operated switch, but you may forget to turn it ON (risking overheating your engine) or forget to turn it OFF (running down your battery). During the installation process, you will set the temperature for when the thermostat turns the

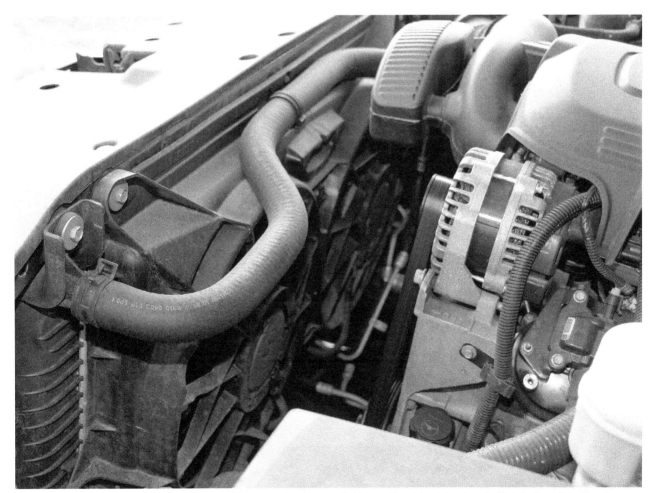

The author's 2008 Chevy Silverado does not use an engine-driven fan, but does have two electric fans with an integral shroud mounted just aft of the radiator. Since the radiator is significantly wider than tall, two fans located side by side pull air through the bulk of the radiator.

fan ON and OFF, so this will be a more consistent method of controlling your engine's water temperature. Common settings for some aftermarket fan relay kits turn the fan ON at 200 degrees F and OFF at 185 degrees F, while others turn the fan ON at 185 degrees F and OFF at 170 degrees F. As mentioned previously, an electric fan draws a lot of current, so to protect the electric fan's switching contacts, a fan relay should be included in the wiring.

POWER DOOR LOCKS

The basics of power door locks are that when you manually operate a switch, electric current runs through wire to a lock actuator that locks or unlocks the door, depending on the position of the switch. Switches for power door locks are typically a toggle or a rocker. Like most everything these days, there are multiple ways to do just about everything, and that includes circuitry for power door locks. The most

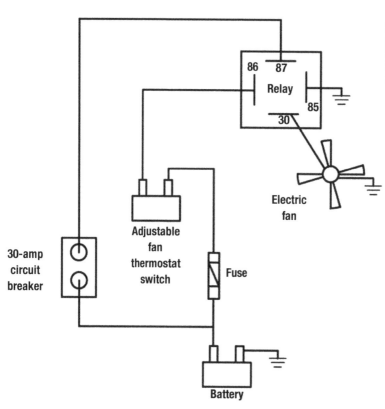

For the most consistent and therefore efficient cooling of your vehicle's engine, an electric fan should be switched ON and OFF by an adjustable thermostat. This will allow the fan to run when it is needed, and shut off when it is not required.

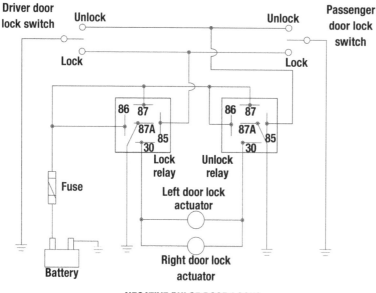

Common in Japanese-manufactured vehicles is the negative-pulse door-lock system. At each door-lock switch is an SPDT center-off switch that is wired in parallel. When a switch is activated, a low-current ground powers the coil of the appropriate relay (lock or unlock).

NEGATIVE PULSE DOOR LOCKS

common switching methods are negative pulse, positive pulse, voltage-reversal rest at ground, and variable voltage. Regardless of manufacturer, door-lock actuators are usually of the two-wire design. What this means is that when power is applied to one wire and the other wire is grounded, the actuator moves to lock the door. To unlock the door, the wires are reversed (the first wire becomes the ground wire and power is applied to the second wire).

While they are not common on late-model vehicles that use power door locks, a hidden emergency switch that unlocks the doors or opens at least one door window is highly recommended. Some late-model vehicles do provide the option of using a traditional keyed door lock in case there is a problem with the remote system.

Both negative-pulse and positive-pulse circuits use two relays, with the difference in wiring being between the switch and the relays. Between the relays and the actuators, wiring is the same. Since relays are used in each of these systems, the current involved is less, so smaller-gauge wiring (18- or 16-gauge) can be used.

In the voltage-reversal rest-at-ground type–circuit, two DPDT (double-pole, double-throw) switches are wired in series. One of these switches will have four wires and be considered the master switch, with the opposite switch having five wires and being considered the slave switch. The master switch can be on either side of the vehicle. All components must be able to endure higher current since no

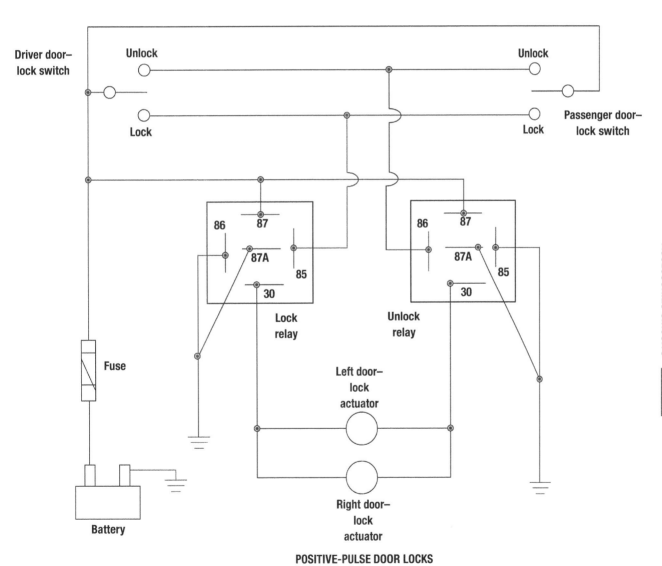

POSITIVE-PULSE DOOR LOCKS

More common in American-manufactured vehicles is the positive-pulse door-lock system. When a switch is activated, +12VDC powers the coil of the appropriate relay (lock or unlock).

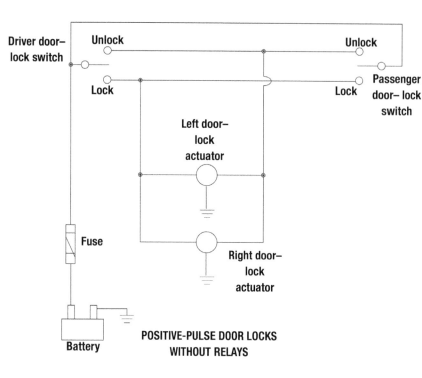

Many older GM vehicles with power door locks used three-wire actuators. They included two coils (one for lock and one for unlock), but did not use relays. Operating the actuators requires between 5 and 10 amps, which requires that the wire size be at least 12-gauge. The switches must be sized accordingly as well.

POSITIVE-PULSE DOOR LOCKS WITHOUT RELAYS

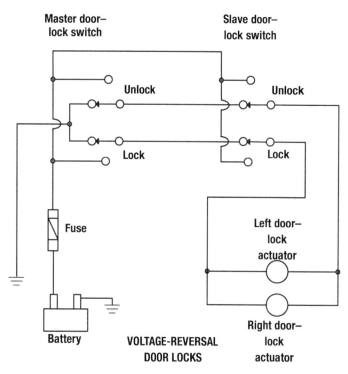

The voltage-reversal rest-at-ground system for door locks uses a pair of DPDT (double-pole double-throw) switches wired in series. When a switch is activated, it sends +12VDC to one of the lock/unlock wires.

VOLTAGE-REVERSAL DOOR LOCKS

relays are used, including the wires, which should be at least 14-gauge, if not 12-gauge.

Variable-voltage circuits use a voltage controller located between the switch and actuator. Signals of varying voltage pass through one wire to the controller. The controller then interprets the voltage level and acts upon that command.

The switching process varies from each manufacturer and even from one vehicle to another. For this simple reason, it is recommended to consult with a vehicle-specific service or repair manual before attempting service to power door-lock circuits.

POWER WINDOWS

Power windows are wired in similar fashion to power door locks, except that power windows can be operated independently of each other. The most common switching

Some vehicles with power windows have the controls located in the center console. This requires just one switch for each window.

A common sight in contemporary vehicles are controls for power mirrors, front windows, rear windows, a window lock, and door locks. Since these controls are located on the driver's door, there is one controller for the driver's window, but two controllers for each additional window (one here and one at each window).

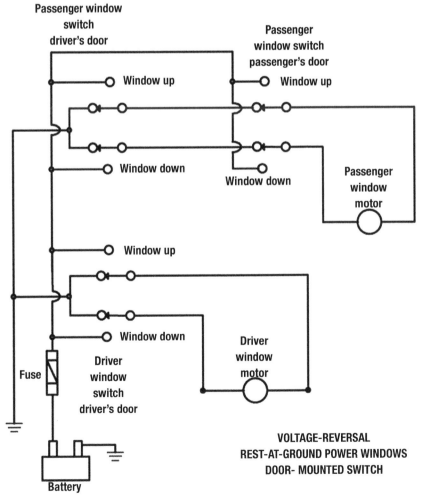

Double-pole double-throw switches are used throughout in the voltage-reversal rest at ground. When door-mounted switches are used, one DPDT switch is used for the driver's window, with two DPDT switches required for each additional power window. One of the two additional switches is typically mounted at the driver's position and the other one near the window that it controls.

VOLTAGE-REVERSAL
REST-AT-GROUND POWER WINDOWS
DOOR- MOUNTED SWITCH

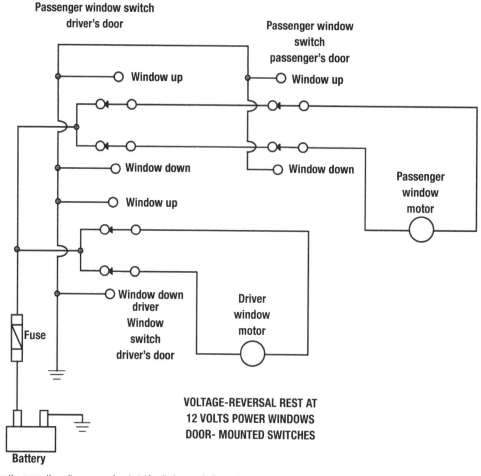

Passenger window switch driver's door

Passenger window switch passenger's door

Window up

Window up

Window down

Window down

Window up

Passenger window motor

Window down driver

Window switch driver's door

Driver window motor

Fuse

VOLTAGE-REVERSAL REST AT 12 VOLTS POWER WINDOWS DOOR- MOUNTED SWITCHES

Battery

As you might guess from the name, the voltage reversal rest at 12 volts is very similar to the voltage reversal at ground, except for the polarity, of course. Since rest is at 12 volts, depressing the switch when the ignition switch is in the IGN/RUN position sends ground to one of the up/down wires, causing the window to move in the corresponding position.

methods are voltage-reversal rest at ground, voltage-reversal rest at 12 volts switched, and voltage-reversal rest open. Since power windows can be operated independently, the location of the switches is what usually determines the circuitry. If the switches are located in the center console, only one switch is required for each window. If the switches are located in the doors, however, one switch is required for the driver's window and two switches are required for each additional power window.

In the voltage-reversal rest-at-ground circuit, movement of the window occurs when 12-volt DC power is sent to the actuator. In a vehicle that has centrally located switches, one DPDT switch is used for each power window. One pole is for the "up" direction, while the other pole is for the "down" direction. If the switches were located in the doors, the driver's window would be operated by one DPDT switch. For each additional power window, two more DPDT switches would be used. One of these would be located in the driver's door and the other located in the door for which the switch is for. Just as in the power-lock circuit, one of these switches will have four wires and be considered the master switch, with

the opposite switch having five wires and being considered the slave switch. The master switch can be on either side of the vehicle, however. All components must be able to endure higher current since no relays are used, including the wires, which should be at least 14-gauge, if not 12-gauge.

A voltage-reversal rest-at-12-volts switched circuit is the same as a voltage-reversal rest-at-ground–type circuit, except that rest is at 12 volts, rather than at ground. This means that window movement occurs when the switch receives ground. This type of circuitry is often used when the switches are mounted in the doors.

Voltage-reversal rest open circuitry is also similar to a voltage-reversal rest at ground circuit. The notable difference is that when the switch is activated, both power and ground are sent to the actuator to raise or lower the window.

The switching process varies from each manufacturer, and even from one vehicle to another. For this simple reason, it is recommended that you consult with a vehicle-specific service or repair manual before attempting service to power-window circuits.

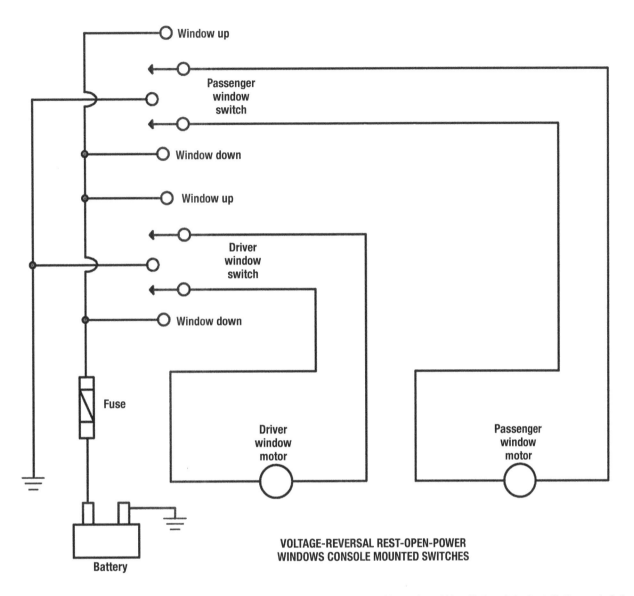

**VOLTAGE-REVERSAL REST-OPEN-POWER
WINDOWS CONSOLE MOUNTED SWITCHES**

Voltage-reversal rest-open-power window circuits are not common, but they are out there. They are used in two-door vehicles with the switches located in the console. Both switches and wires rest at open, so when the switch is activated, both power and ground are sent to the motor.

POWER SEATS

Power seats are available in a variety of configurations: two-way, four-way, six-way, and now even eight-way. Two-way power seats simply move the seat forward or backward. Four-way power seats typically, but not always, added the ability to tilt the seat cushion and seat back forward or backward. This was better than the simple two-way, but still kept the seat cushion and seat back in the same relation to each other. Six-way power seats allow the front of the seat cushion to be raised or lowered, the seat back tilted forward or backward, and the entire seat moved forward or backward. Eight-way power seats are the same as six-way, but also allow for the back of the seat cushion to be raised or lowered.

Power-seat mechanisms vary between manufacturers, sometimes including one motor and a separate clutch system for each axis of movement, or may include one motor for each axis of movement. Since mechanisms and systems are so varied, consult a vehicle-specific manual for instructions on how to service power seats in your vehicle.

AUXILIARY FUSE PANELS

If you want to add electric accessories to your vehicle, but don't want to mess around with the vehicle's original fuse panel, or if it is already full, a common solution to the problem is adding an auxiliary fuse panel. These are available through most any major auto parts house that carries wiring components and are easy to install. Auxiliary fuse panels typically have between three and eight circuits, as they are designed to provide power for accessories only. Of these circuits, a certain number of them will be constant hot circuits, while the rest will be ignition hot circuits. Constant hot means that the accessory connected to this circuit could be used at any time, while an ignition hot circuit requires that the engine be running in order to use any accessories on that circuit.

After securely mounting the auxiliary fuse panel to a convenient location, connect a positive and a negative wire between the vehicle's battery and the power and ground terminals on the auxiliary fuse panel. Be sure to read and follow the instructions provided with your auxiliary fuse panel for specific connection procedures. Adding electric accessories is then done in the same manner as if they were powered by the vehicle's main fuse panel.

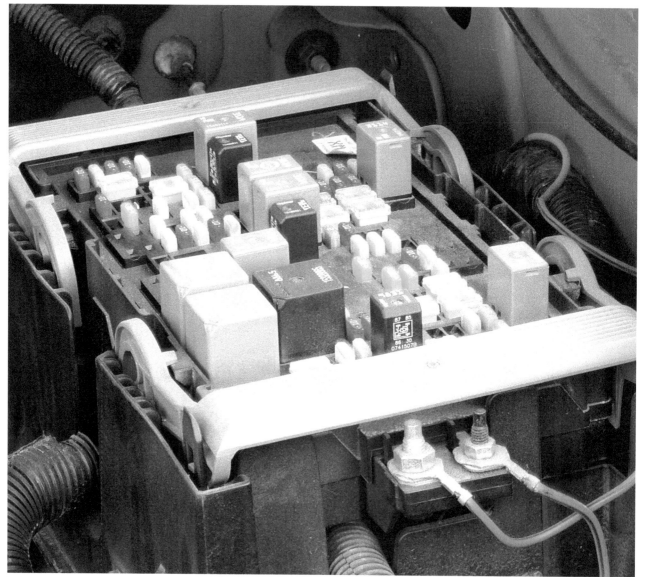

Under the hood of the author's late-model pickup is an auxiliary fuse panel. In addition to numerous fuses of varying capacities, there are also several relays. With the ever-increasing number of electrical circuits in today's vehicles, auxiliary fuse panels are becoming more common. Basic functions are still located in the main panel, but optional power accessories are commonly relegated to the auxiliary panel.

Chapter 7
Audio and Video Applications

Not all that long ago, installing an aftermarket stereo in your vehicle simply meant that you purchased a radio and a pair of speakers, plugged them in, and were done. You could get that done on a Saturday morning, wash and wax the car in the afternoon, and still have time to pick up your best gal that evening.

Car audio certainly has changed over the years, giving us so many more choices. Not just choosing one brand over another, but choices of broadcast sources and prerecorded media. Audio is not the only choice anymore either, as now we have the availability of video presentation and navigation systems.

AUDIO

Car audio can be as simple or as exotic as you desire and your budget allows. The perfect system is what provides you with what you want. The original AM radio that was in the 1968 Chevrolet pickup that serves as the basis for a vehicle-specific wiring kit installation in the next chapter had an integral speaker. The only connections to be made were

one for power and another for a radio antenna. That, no doubt, is about as simple as it gets. Much better sound is not too complicated than that, however, and is still affordable.

Upgrading from that simple AM radio would include the addition of an AM/FM/CD player. That would allow you to listen to AM and FM broadcasts and play your favorite CDs. Most, but not all, of these stereos will also allow you to play MP3 discs, while some will also play Windows Media Audio (WMA) files, as well. These last two formats allow you to burn CDs of your favorite collections of music on your computer and then play them in your car. Many of these stereos will also be compatible with your iPod. Other options to consider when designing your vehicle's audio system include being able to tune in to HD radio or satellite broadcasts.

Once you choose the source of your music, the next step is determining how good you want it to sound. The quality of that sound will be based most notably upon the speakers but will also be affected by amplifiers and subwoofers.

The old AM radio out of my '68 Chevy pickup was pretty basic: a wire for power and an antenna lead. From the best I can tell, the speaker was built into the radio, as I could not find any connection terminals for external speakers.

This dorsal fin antenna atop a vehicle is an indication that the vehicle is equipped with satellite radio. The antenna cable feeds through a hole in the roof panel, then runs down one of the windshield pillars, and then connects to the back of the satellite radio unit.

The OEM satellite radio in the author's Chevy Silverado is not as colorful as many of the aftermarket radios that are available, but it does provide the same information and is easy to read. The radio display indicates what station is being played, the artist, and the time. By pressing the "I" information button, other info can be displayed. At the lower right corner is a jack for plugging in an iPod.

Stereo Receiver

Your choice of a stereo depends on whether you are replacing an existing system in your vehicle or installing a stereo in a newly constructed or restored vehicle. If you have the benefit of having an existing stereo system your choices will be easier, as you simply need to determine what kinds of improvements you desire to make with your upgrade. If you do not have the luxury of an existing system to establish a baseline, your efforts toward creating a perfect system may be trial and error.

Although factory receivers are not always the best, they are typically of better quality than the OEM speakers, so if you purchase a new receiver, you will most likely require new speakers as well. Unless you are purchasing a new receiver

Although we cannot actually see the speakers or their electrical connections, you can bet that the sounds from the stereo in this sedan delivery can really rock. Do not forget to eliminate any unnecessary vibrations in your vehicle, insulate as much as possible, and upholster everything that you can to get the best sound.

primarily for other features such as iPod-compatibility or USB connections, you might want to begin your car audio upgrade with new speakers first to see if that meets your need.

Speakers

OEM speakers are typically made of cheap paper-based materials that distort and deteriorate after time. So even if your speakers sounded good when the vehicle was new, you may have noticed degradation in sound quality over the years.

Aftermarket speakers are more durable because they are made of higher-quality material. This also allows them to provide more realistic reproduction of the sounds coming from your receiver. Speakers can be designed as either full-range or component-based. Full-range speakers have some combination of tweeter, midrange, and woofer capabilities, making them an economical upgrade from OEM speakers. Component-based speakers use separate woofers and tweeters to provide the greatest separation of sound levels. Since multiple components are required, this type of system requires more space within the vehicle and typically costs more.

Amplifier

If you really like to crank up the music, an amplifier will allow you to do so without distorting the sound. Using an amplifier will provide clearer, crisper sound and detail at all volume levels, which is especially good if you like to drive around with the windows open or the top down.

Wiring It All Together

Since this is a wiring book rather than a stereo book, discussion of how to make it all work is more important than what components you feel that you need. You should disconnect the ground cable from the battery before doing any electrical work on your vehicle. Just be sure to reconnect this ground wire to the battery terminal before you expect your new stereo to work. Also read any and all installation instructions provided with your new stereo components to make sure that you do not do anything that will void any warranties.

If you are merely dealing with a receiver and one or two pairs of speakers, the wiring requirements are straightforward. The receiver will typically have two wires coming out the back of it: a power wire and a ground wire. Simply connect the power wire from the receiver to your vehicle's fuse panel. Most all fuse panels will have a terminal specified for use with a stereo. Some receivers will also have a wire that should be connected to a keyed ignition source, which allows the radio to be ON only when the vehicle is running or the ignition switch is in ACC position. Then connect the ground wire to a suitable ground source. You will also need to connect the radio antenna. This will be either to a designated female plug on a pigtail or directly to a port on the receiver's housing. Wires to your speakers will run directly from the back of the receiver to each speaker. The receiver will probably have bass, treble, and fade controls at a minimum, so verify that speaker wires are connected to their corresponding speakers for these controls to work properly. In this situation, the speaker can be connected by using 16- or 18-gauge multi-strand copper wire.

If you add an amplifier to your audio system, the amplifier should be powered directly from the battery and will also require a suitable ground as well. RCA cables from the RCA output terminals on the back of the receiver should run to the RCA input terminals on the amplifier. Speakers are then wired in series by running a speaker wire from the + (plus) output terminal on the amplifier to the + side on the first speaker. Then run a speaker wire from the - (minus) side of the first speaker to the + side on the next speaker. Continue this for each speaker, connecting the - side of the last speaker back to the - output terminal of the amplifier. Note that wiring the speakers in parallel (pluses to pluses and minuses to minuses) would offer very low resistance and could eventually fry your amplifier. If you are using more than two sets of speakers, you should consider using a four channel (or higher) amplifier, or multiple amplifiers.

For audio systems that use multiple amplifiers or subwoofers, it would be prudent to install a secondary battery (and modify the charging system accordingly) to power the second and successive amplifiers. Since this would be a high-current situation, you may need to use relays to provide power to individual components as required. Also, larger-gauge speaker cables should be used.

On this GM OEM satellite radio, sound controls are accessed by pressing the center button of the knob at the upper right. You then select the variable that you want to adjust by pressing the button beneath the appropriate tab, and then turn the upper right knob clockwise or counterclockwise until the desired setting is achieved.

To prevent the need to butcher the stock dash in this 1969 Camaro to install a new stereo, a marine stereo unit is being used and will be mounted in the trunk. The marine stereo is operated via a wired controller that is approximately 4 inches in diameter and mounted within the console between the two bucket seats. A wireless remote can also be used to operate the stereo.

The controller includes a digital readout screen and all of the controls necessary to select radio stations, raise or lower volume, or myriad other choices. It is wired to the stereo unit in the trunk via a cable that runs from the controller, down through the console, under the seats, into the trunk, and on to the stereo. When the console is closed, no one knows that there is a stereo in the vehicle.

Using otherwise wasted space is the stereo installed vertically between the trunk opening and the left rear quarter panel. A sub-amp is then secured to a board that is cut to fit as a block-off plate between the accessible and hidden portions of the trunk.

This shows how the sub-amp panel will fit into place. It and the rest of the trunk will be upholstered to match the interior of the car.

The main amplifier is mounted in the block-off panel on the passenger side of the trunk in similar fashion to the sub-amp.

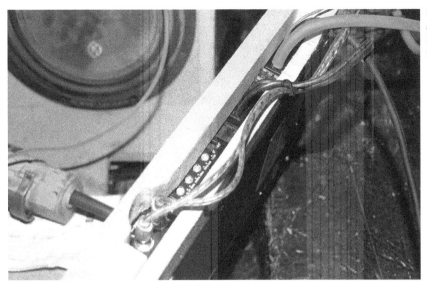

Mounting of the amplifier allows for connecting and disconnecting all cables, but will otherwise be upholstered to match the rest of the trunk-mounted components.

Speakers are mounted in trunk-mounted enclosures, along with the battery. Overall, this is a clean, simple method of installing a stereo without butchering the dash. For more information on car audio systems, refer to *How to Install Automotive Mobile Electronic Systems* by Jason Syner (Motorbooks, 2009).

VIDEO

Two reasons for installing an in-dash video monitor in your vehicle are for system control of the stereo and for GPS navigation. A larger screen simply makes stereo settings and other menu selections easier to see. Additionally, when combined with a GPS navigation system, touch-screen controls are much more accessible and therefore safer. While a bigger screen is easier to see, having a higher-resolution makes the image sharper.

GPS

Depending on the system you choose, there are two or three major components of an in-dash navigation system. The two basics are a stereo with a built-in screen and an external GPS antenna. The optional component is a remotely located connection box, which is where audio and video inputs and outputs are located.

Besides standard power and ground electrical connections, the navigation system may require a connection to the vehicle speed sensor (VSS) wire. For some navigation systems to work properly, they must know how fast the vehicle is moving in order to accurately tell you to "turn left in 2.1 miles." When the vehicle is in motion, the VSS wire sends from 800 to approximately 1,000 pulses per mile. If the navigation system is not connected to the VSS, it will not detect if the vehicle is moving or not. In similar fashion, some systems also require an electrical connection to the back-up light signal so that the navigation system can compensate for the vehicle moving backward. Newer navigation systems simply rely on the GPS satellite information to track a vehicle. If your navigation system requires connection to the VSS or back-up lights, refer to a vehicle-specific manual to find and identify these connections.

The GPS antenna works best if mounted outside of the vehicle, with the roof or deck lid giving the best results. Since navigation communication is done by satellite, you must remember that a GPS antenna cannot "see" through metal and should not be located inside a vehicle with windows that are equipped with an electric window defroster, metallic window tint, solar reflective material, or a windshield-mounted radio antenna. Although GPS antenna cables are inserted through a hole in the roof from the factory, aftermarket installations typically route the cable through a rear window or door seal.

OTHER CONSIDERATIONS

Regardless of how much money you spend on quality audio, visual, or navigation equipment, you will not get the most out of it if your vehicle is extraordinarily noisy. Unwanted noise can come from wind whistling through worn weather stripping around doors and windows or from vibrations in the vehicle. New weather stripping is affordable and is fairly easy to install. Since all vehicles have some natural vibration noise at various harmonics, installing vibration-dampening material may be a good investment to enhance your stereo installation.

Chapter 8
Wiring Installations

There may be a variety of reasons for completely rewiring a vehicle: restoration of a vehicle to like-new (or at least drivable) condition, part of a new street-driven vehicle's construction, or part of a non-street-legal vehicle's construction. There are also various ways to go about wiring any of those vehicles. The idea is to do so in the most efficient and effective way.

Multiple companies provide vehicle-specific kits for several vehicles originally manufactured during the 1960s and 1970s. If you are working on a vehicle that could use an updated version of a stock wiring harness, this could be the best route to follow. Since the automotive aftermarket is ever expanding, you may be able to find a vehicle-specific kit for your vehicle, even if it is not from within those two decades.

Even more companies manufacture universal wiring kits. These would be suitable for a vehicle restoration for which a vehicle-specific kit is not available. Different kits are available that have varying numbers of circuits, so whether you are rewiring a street-legal vehicle or a race car, this is usually a great place to start.

If you are wiring a vehicle that is not supported by the automotive aftermarket, you desire to implement purely custom electronic circuits, or you simply feel really adventurous, you can wire a vehicle from scratch. You can start with a catalog from your favorite electrical supply house and design your own custom system.

WHEN TO SOLDER AND WHEN TO CRIMP

While soldering electrical connections was the common practice for so many years, solderless (crimp-on) connectors have somewhat made soldering a lost art. As long as you perform either method correctly, they both will perform satisfactorily.

One situation in particular where soldering will come in handy is when adding a connector to a large wire (4-gauge or larger) such as battery cables. These can be crimped on, but they require an expensive crimping tool that you most likely will not use often unless you wire vehicles every day.

If you have access to a propane or MAPP gas torch and 60/40 lead-based rosin core solder, you can do this yourself. Simply strip enough insulation off the cable so that about ⅛ inch extends past the metal part of the terminal. Clamp the cable in a vise so that the strands are exposed and the terminal slips down over them. Heat the terminal and the cable with the blue flame of the torch until the solder begins to flow into the connection. Remove the heat and allow the connection to cool.

PROJECT 1
Vehicle-Specific Kits

 More info: Dennis@hot-rod-garage.com

 Time: Less than 40 hours actual time spent.

 Cost: Between $400 and $500, depending on vehicle and manufacturer of wiring kit.

 Key Concept: One source for all wiring.

 Number of People: One person.

 Skill Level: Fairly easy if you can read directions and know which components are which.

 Tip: Read the directions a couple of times before starting, to become familiar with the process.

 Warning: Take your time, re-read the instructions if in doubt, and always make sure that your connections are good.

 Parts: Vehicle-specific wiring kit.

 Tools: Wire strippers, crimpers, test light, and multimeter (if available).

For many vehicles (typically 1960s or newer), various manufacturers are creating replacement wiring harnesses. After all, these vehicles commonly have most if not all of the creature comforts that contemporary vehicles have. The original wiring is getting old, which is not necessarily a problem. But connections are getting weak, and in many cases, previous owners may have put in a few too many splices while adding this or that and you simply don't feel comfortable with the existing wiring harness. If you have a vehicle that you feel could benefit from new wiring and a vehicle-specific kit is available for your application, this is a great way to go.

A vehicle-specific kit will provide you with all of the wires necessary for your vehicle. For some applications, you may be required to splice specific plugs and connectors from your existing wiring onto the new wire, but this is easy enough to do. With this type of kit, you still have the option of modifying the wiring and connectors to fit aftermarket gauges or other nonstock accessories.

For this section of this book, I installed a vehicle-specific kit from Painless Performance Products (also called Painless Wiring) into my 1968 Chevrolet C10 pickup. One of the first things I noticed about this kit is that it includes lots of wire options that my truck does not have, such as power windows, power door locks, cargo light, and third brake light. The kit includes wires that are already terminated within the fuse panel, so unlike a custom fuse panel that would allow me to simply leave the unnecessary wire out of the installation, these extra wires will be secured out of the way and out of sight. They will be available if I choose to add those extra options later. It will always be easier to tie unnecessary wires out of the way than to add circuits later.

Painless Performance Products (commonly known as Painless Wiring) manufactures vehicle-specific wiring kits for a growing number of vehicles. If you are looking for a wiring harness that is similar to stock as far as accessories, a vehicle-specific kit is the way to go. However, you may have more wire than you need if you are working on a base model vehicle that did not have all of the available options.

At the heart of the kit is the fuse panel (18 circuits in this case), wiring for components inside the cab, wiring for components outside the cab, connectors, instructions, and a few other miscellaneous items.

Although it was not the primary reason for completely rewiring the truck, the existing alternator was faulty, so now is the time to replace it. It is a GM three-wire alternator, but it will be replaced by a one-wire unit.

4

The back of the stock three-wire alternator includes the alternator charge stud and two other connections. These other two connections are for the ignition sense and the battery sense. For simplicity, I'll replace this alternator with a one-wire unit.

5

This photo of the front of the alternator clearly shows that the pulley is for a serpentine belt. Since that is the type of pulley on the crankshaft as well, that is what will be needed on the replacement alternator.

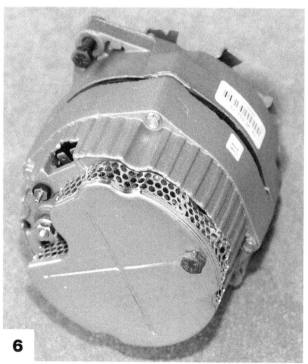

6

This replacement alternator can be used as a one-wire or as a three-wire, depending on how it is wired. The alternator charge stud will be used in either situation. The necessary terminals for ignition sense and the battery sense are there to use if desired, but for simplicity, I followed the instructions for using the one-wire alternator option.

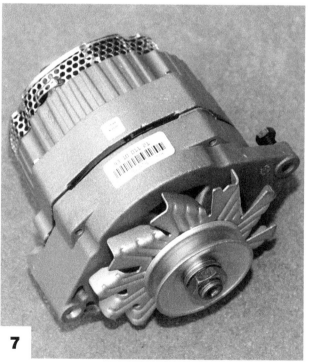

7

Alas, my new alternator is equipped with a pulley for a standard V-belt. An impact wrench and the appropriate-sized socket make quick work of swapping the two pulleys, however. A benefit of working with the same auto parts store on a regular basis is that they allow me to switch pulleys as required.

The main collection of wires into the engine compartment simply plugs into the stock fuse panel through the firewall. As with many vehicles that have had more than one owner, there are multiple wires extending out of various other holes in the firewall, along with various forms of tape or convoluted tubing being used to protect the wires.

8

This photo shows the stock electrical connection to one of the headlights. The plug can simply be pulled off the spade terminals of the headlamp. This wiring kit includes new headlamp plugs, but these plugs could be reused and wired into the system if necessary.

9

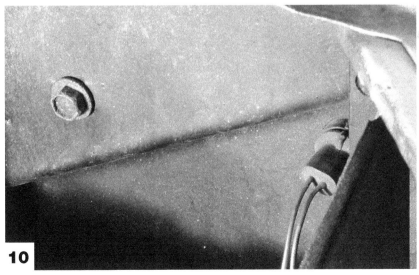

This photo shows the electrical connection to the right front turn signal light and the stock ground connection for the headlight on that side slightly to the left. As you can see, the sheet metal that the ground wire would be connected to is somewhat rusty and does not provide the best ground. A better method of grounding is discussed in Chapter 2, Ground (Return Path).

10

This is a look at the stock fuse panel with its outdated glass fuses. As seen in this photo, additional accessory circuits have been added by connecting to the available spade terminals that are designed for that purpose. The two silver cans are flashers used for the turn signals and the hazard flashers.

This close-up photo of the engine compartment side of the fuse panel shows that some wires are missing, the wiring is not very tidy, and the wires look brittle. None of this is a good thing.

To eliminate as much confusion as possible, it is best to remove all existing wiring that will not be used before adding any new wiring. On this type of fuse panel that protrudes through the firewall, a bolt passes through the outside portion and threads into a nut fixed within the inside portion of the fuse panel. Remove this bolt and then unplug the outside portion from the inside portion.

The red wires near the center of the photo pass between the distributor and an ignition control box mounted on the right inner fender. Besides these wires not being connected to the proper terminals, they were routed haphazardly and not fully protected by the convoluted tubing that was there to protect them.

This is the stock connection between the fuse panel and the steering column wiring (turn signals, horn, and so on). The two-piece connection can be pulled apart, leaving the stock wiring within the stock steering column. Just as with the headlight plugs, the connector could be used if necessary and, depending on the vehicle, may not be available, so don't be so quick to discard it.

To remove the dash panel, it will be necessary to remove the knobs from the headlight switch and the windshield wiper (as well as any others that might be on your particular vehicle). The knobs may include a set screw that will need to be loosened. After the knob is removed, the bezel nut will also need to be removed.

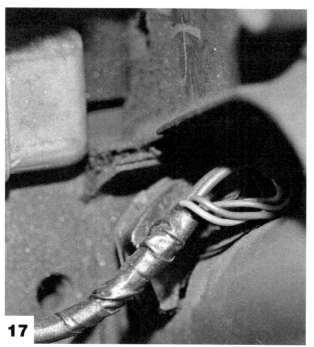

17

Looking through the dash where the dash panel has been removed, we see a circuit breaker for the horn at the upper left and ignition-switch wires passing over the steering column. The ignition-switch wires connect to the fuse panel to the left and the ignition switch to the right. Before removing any wires, it is a good idea to make note of where they were originally so you will have a better idea of where to route the new wires. Verify that you avoid anything that will pinch wires or cause other mechanisms to bind.

18

Looking through the dash where the dash panel has been removed, we can see a portion of the stock fuse panel, the drive cable for the mechanical speedometer, and the circuit breaker for the horn. To remove the speedometer cable, I unthreaded one end from the transmission and then cut the end off the cable, rather than attempt to pass it through a grommet in the firewall.

19

As seen by etchings on the outside of the firewall, the new fuse panel is slightly larger than the stock unit. A pneumatic saw would work wonders to enlarge the hole, but I did not have access to one. I made do by drilling several holes and "connecting the dots" with a cutoff wheel and a die grinder.

20

With the fuse panel in place on the interior side of the firewall, the exterior side of the fuse panel can be plugged into it and then secured by installing a bolt. Having an assistant to hold the interior side while you plug in and secure the exterior side will make this much easier.

21

With both portions of the new fuse panel secured together, holes can be drilled for the two mounting bolts. With bolts, flat washers, and nuts at opposite corners of the fuse panel, it is securely in place. A heavy plastic wire tie was used to bundle the engine compartment wires together near the fuse panel before they are routed to their destinations.

22

Although few wires, if any, will actually pass beneath the seat of the truck, it quickly made sense to remove the seat before attempting to do any work beneath the dash. The stock gas tank will be removed eventually, but for now was left in place.

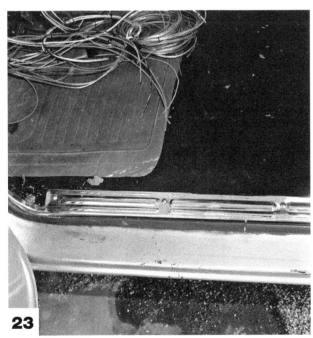

23

Rather than take a chance on ruining the carpet by rolling around on it and potentially ripping it, I decided to remove it too. Simply remove the four screws holding each of the doorsill plates, remove the plates, and lift the carpeting out. This will also eliminate the need to pick all of the tiny pieces of stripped wiring insulation out of the carpet.

24

Let the new wiring begin! All of the wiring lying under the steering wheel gets routed somewhere and connected to something. A benefit of the Painless Wiring kit is that all wires are labeled (approximately every 12 inches) as to what section of wiring they belong in and what they get connected to.

25

The next step is to begin routing wires to wherever they are to be connected. It is necessary to think ahead about what additional components may be installed that the wire will be required to go around.

26

In any wiring kit that comes with wires preterminated at the fuse panel, the installer will be required to deal with bunches of wires, whether those wires are required or not. In the kit from Painless, the wires are labeled and are bundled in groups. Those bundles, however, will need to be broken down further by the installer.

27

Wires running into the engine compartment include wires that connect to the starter, alternator, headlights, parking lights, front turn signals, choke, electric fan, and distributor.

28

Before connecting any of the wires, continue subdividing the large bundles until each wire is routed at least approximately to its intended connection point. Use wire ties to bind these smaller groups of wires together in their more accurate bundles.

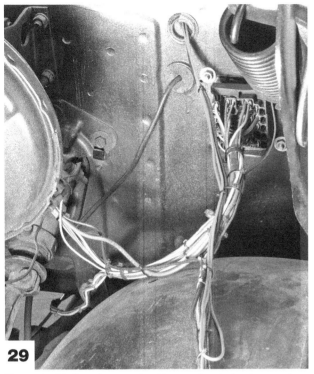

29

Wires running into the engine compartment have now been broken down, running into one of three basic directions: forward toward the lights, downward toward the starter (or rear of the vehicle), and upward toward the rear of the engine.

30

A portion of the wires routed around the rear of the engine includes those that terminate at the distributor. Since these wires will be cut considerably shorter than what they are, I simply tied them off with a disposable bread tie for the time being.

This small bundle includes wire for the electric choke, temperature sender, oil-pressure sender, horn, and air-conditioning compressor. Since none of the wires are being connected at this time, it will be easier to reroute any of them later if desired.

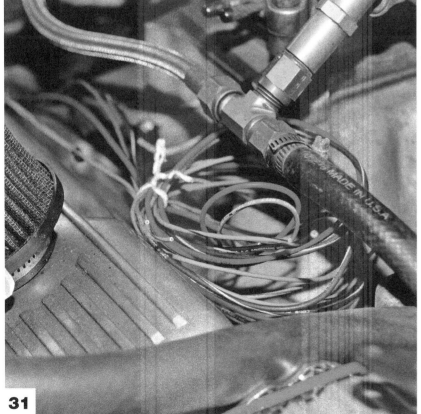

31

32

Wires for the taillights, brake lights, fuel pump, and fuel-level sender were routed down the front of the firewall, over to the driver's-side frame rail, and then back to the rear of the vehicle. In pickup trucks, verify that the routing of wires (other than simply disconnecting wires at their terminal points) does not prevent the truck bed from being removed.

33

The condition of the existing starter was suspect, so it was removed and tested at the local auto parts store. Sure enough, it needed to be replaced, so now was the best time to do that.

34

It is unknown whether the burn on the battery cable to the starter is the cause or result of the starter failure. Either way, that cable needs to be replaced. The existing ignition-switch wire has a few too many splices in it as well.

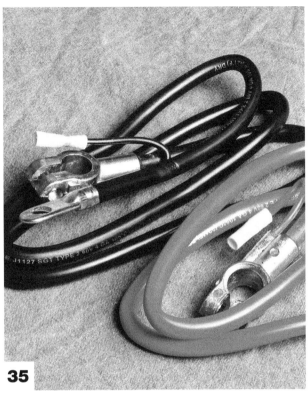

35

I determined what length the new battery cables needed to be and then had them made up at my local NAPA store. Off-the-shelf cables are available at most auto parts stores, but for just slightly more, I could get custom cables made to the exact length I wanted them. Some parts stores offer battery cables in only one color. If you find this to be the case, you can use red or black heat shrink tubing or electrical tape on one cable or the other to differentiate the negative from the positive.

36

These yellow wires are for optional power door locks and power windows that my truck does not have. In this situation, we have the choice of cutting these wires out of the harness or simply wrapping them up and stashing them out of the way. Since there is always the possibility of adding these optional accessories, I'll stash the wires. If the wires were not already connected to the fuse panel at the factory, the wire could be left in a storage box and then added later if desired.

37

Since the ignition switch seems to work okay as is, I'll leave it in place and simply connect the multi-wire plug to the back side of it. If the ignition switch were faulty or otherwise required replacement, it would need to be pulled outward from the dash after disconnecting the wiring. You should consult with a vehicle-specific service manual to determine how to remove the ignition switch.

38

All of the dust and dirt on this ignition switch indicate that this is the original. The new switch included in the kit looks basically the same (albeit without the dust and dirt) and plugs into the original switch.

Being able to remove the dash panel makes access to the fuse panel and routing wires behind the dash much easier than with the dash panel in place. Use wire ties to keep wires that have not yet been routed out of your way.

39

40

This truck did not have a dimmer switch when I took possession of it. The previous owner said that it was too difficult to install. Actually, installing a dimmer switch is quite easy: connect the power wire from the headlight switch to the single terminal on the dimmer switch. Connect one wire to one of the lower two terminals and to the high-beam light circuit and then connect another wire to the remaining terminal and to the low-beam light circuit. Then mount the dimmer switch to the floor with two bolts that in this case thread into nuts that are already welded to the floor.

41

A neutral safety switch is a great safety feature on any vehicle. On this automatic-transmission–equipped vehicle, it is mounted near the base of the steering column. Vehicles with manual transmissions have a similar feature that is activated by depressing the clutch pedal. This neutral safety switch also includes terminals for the back-up lights, but those will not be used for this vehicle.

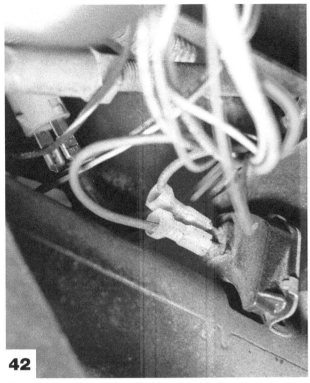

42

One purple wire connects to each of the two neutral safety terminals to allow the engine to start only when the transmission is in PARK or NEUTRAL. Just beyond the neutral safety switch are the two electrical terminals and wires for the brake light switch.

43

By removing the pipe plug (with the orange paint in the threads), the water-temperature sender can be threaded into the cylinder head. This location will give a more accurate (real-world) temperature than if it were located near the thermostat housing or anywhere else on the intake manifold. Be ready for some engine coolant to pour out when you remove this plug.

44

Due to the difference in size between the temperature sender and the opening in the cylinder head, a brass fitting was required between the two to make up the difference. On both sets of threads (the sender into the fitting and the fitting into the cylinder head) Teflon tape must be used to prevent leakage of engine coolant.

45

Remove the plug, thread the temperature sender in by hand to avoid cross-threading it, and then finish tightening it with a wrench. Then remove the thumbscrew from the tip of the sender, place the wire connector of the water-temperature gauge or warning light over the stud, and then secure with a correct size nut when you cannot find the thumbscrew that you dropped.

The oil-pressure sender threads into a pressurized oil galley access hole in the engine block. In this application, both a reducer and an elbow were required to fit the sender into where it needed to be. After installing the sender into the block, the wiring connection is the same as with the water-temperature sender.

46

The stock fuel tank in this vintage truck is located in the cab behind the seat. The original fuel-level sender wire is seen running down along the front of the tank and continues under the seat and up to the back side of the dash. The tube coming out of the tank is what the fuel line to the carburetor would be connected to. As part of this project, a new poly-fuel tank was installed beneath the bed, behind the rear axle. More importantly, it was relocated outside the cab.

47

A new fuel tank was located beneath the truck bed between the frame rails. This necessitated relocating the electric fuel pump as well as routing wires for the fuel pump and the fuel-level sender along the driver's-side frame rail with the rear light wires to the back of the truck.

48

WIRING INSTALLATIONS

104

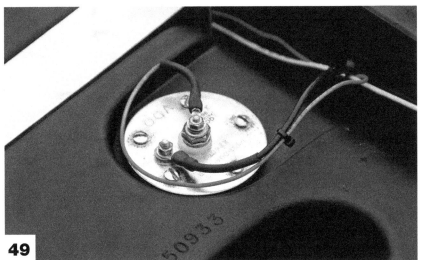

After fuel tank relocation was completed and wires run, connections were made to the fuel pump and fuel-level sender. The red wire attaches to the fuel-level sender and runs forward to the fuel-level gauge in the dash. The fuel-level sender is grounded by the black wire that runs to a ground stud located in the rear crossmember. The yellow wire connects to the fuel pump relay to the left and to the fuel pump to the right.

49

Stock taillights for this particular truck were round but were hung from the rear stake pockets of the bed via a bracket. They had been removed by the previous owner. Their replacement taillights that were mounted in the rear of the fenders were simply unacceptable, so these Chevrolet HHR taillights were installed.

50

Wiring for the Chevrolet HHR taillights was simple enough and much like any other taillight, having one wire for each taillight and brake light, turn signal, and a ground. Connections can be made with butt connectors for a permanent connection or with bullet connectors to allow for quick disconnect should the bed need to be removed.

51

52

The Painless Wiring kit includes a power wire running from the fuse panel to the electric choke (if used). Just like all other electric accessories, the choke requires a ground also. The black (ground) wire runs to a ground stud mounted on the passenger-side inner fender panel.

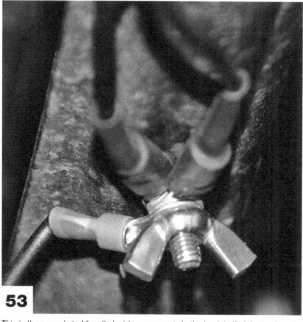

53

This is the ground stud for all electric components in the back half of the truck and is located in the rear crossmember of the vehicle's frame. A wire located above the crossmember connects to the negative battery cable at the battery post connection and establishes the ground stud as a ground. Accessory ground wires are secured to the stud with a wing nut.

54

In similar fashion, this ground stud serves the engine compartment and front lights. The ground stud passes through a hole in the inner fender panel and is secured by one nut. The wire from the negative terminal of the battery is secured by a second nut. Accessory ground wires are secured by the wing nut.

55

At this point, some wiring is completed, while other portions are not. We see wires for the three ground studs connected at the negative battery cable terminal. In similar fashion, power for the MSD ignition box is powered directly by the smaller wire connected to the positive battery cable terminal. The stock heater box still needs to be removed to make room for the Vintage Air air conditioning, heat, and defrost unit. The green wire below the air filter will power the air-conditioning compressor when it is installed, which will also require the alternator to be relocated to the driver's side.

56

The stock wiper motor was an electric unit, which was vastly superior to the old-style vacuum wiper motor found on older vehicles. Still, the wiper motor was upgraded to a bolt-in replacement from New Port Engineering. This new unit has two speeds and includes an optional windshield washer pump.

57

The New Port Engineering wiper motor switch mounts in the aluminum dash and includes wiring that is preterminated in a plug that corresponds to that of the motor, making wiring extremely easy. This product is vehicle-specific, which requires the optional dash bezel extension when used with the stock dash panel.

58

After inserting the wiper switch shaft through the dash, secure it to the aluminum dash panel with the bezel nut. Then slide the control knob over the shaft and secure it with a setscrew.

59

Part of the New Port Engineering wiper motor upgrade was the optional windshield washer pump. Simply attach the mounting bracket to a suitable location (the radiator support in this case), and connect the washer fluid transfer hoses to the reservoir, the pump, and the spray nozzles. Then connect to a power and a ground and you are done. Just verify that the spray nozzles are aimed properly.

60

The final wiring chore of this installation is the various wiring for the air conditioning, heat, and defrost. An additional connection will be to the air-conditioning compressor located in the engine compartment. When the wiring is completed, the wires will be tied up out of sight and the new glove box and glove box door installed.

PROJECT 2
Universal Wiring Kits

 More info: Dennis@hot-rod-garage.com

 Time: Less than 40 hours actual time spent.

 Cost: Between $300 and $500, depending on manufacturer of wiring kit.

 Key Concept: One source for all wiring.

 Number of People: One person.

 Skill Level: Fairly easy if you can read directions and know which components are which.

 Tip: Read the directions a couple of times before starting, to become familiar with the process.

 Warning: Take your time, re-read the instructions if in doubt, and always make sure that your connections are good.

 Parts: Universal wiring kit.

 Tools: Wire strippers, crimpers, test light, multimeter (if available), and screwdrivers.

My previous automotive wiring experience comes from installing a universal-style wiring kit into two different vehicles, the first a 1951 Chevrolet pickup that had been converted from 6-volt to 12-volt by the previous owner in less than grand fashion, and more recently in a ground-up hot rod project. In both of those wiring projects, I used a Wiremaster kit from Affordable Street Rods.

Making a living as a technical writer, I know that directions for commercial products can range from excellent to the other side of useless. All too often, directions become way too complicated for the intended audience. Rich Fox at Affordable Street Rods has made wiring a hot rod easy. The instructions included with the Wiremaster kit are on one side of a piece of 8.5x11-inch paper, with some detail schematics and some company information on the other side. When the directions are this compact, you can be sure that installation is simple. Of course, Fox is available on the other end of the telephone at just about any time, should you have a question.

Two panels are available for street-driven vehicles (another panel is intended primarily for race or off-road applications). The Wiremaster Power Panel II includes circuits for all of the basic wiring in a hot rod; the Wiremaster Power Panel has additional circuits for air conditioning, electric fan, power seats, power windows, electric fuel pump, and additional accessory circuits. Most automotive wiring companies offer a couple of wiring panels: One is designed for a bare-bones hot rod, while others include more circuits for creature comforts. No matter whose wiring panel you choose, it is better to determine as accurately as possible which electrical circuits you will need and then purchase accordingly. Wiring is not difficult, but it isn't something that you want to do halfway and then realize that you don't have an appropriate circuit and be required to retrofit a different panel, although it is possible. If you know that you are going to be running air conditioning, power seats, an electric fuel pump, or other similar electrical components, go ahead and start with a bigger electrical panel.

Wiring your hot rod using either of the Wiremaster kits allows you to complete as much wiring as necessary to get the vehicle operating to the point you desire, and then wire in other accessories later as they are installed. After mounting the panel, color-coded and numbered wires are connected to the like numbered terminals, and then routed to and connected to the appropriate accessory, making for easy installation.

1

For many hot rods, the most suitable location seems to be under the dash, on the inside of the firewall, but on the passenger side. Inside the cowl would be the least susceptible to weather and would be as convenient as possible for wiring or replacing fuses.

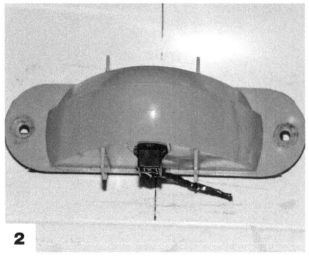

2

A third brake light unit from a Dodge Neon was installed above the deck lid. When scrounging the salvage yards for lighting accessories, be sure that you get any necessary plugs and enough wiring to connect to: simply two wires to connect, a power wire from the fuse panel, and a ground wire.

3

The third brake light lay closer to horizontal than vertical, but with the lines of the roadster body, there wasn't much choice. The upholstery material of the seat back rolls over the rear of the body somewhat, removing the possibility of moving the light forward and more vertical.

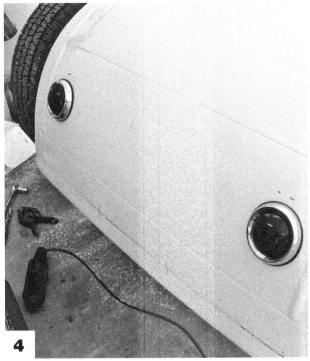

4

Taillights from a 1950 Pontiac that are flush mounted and about 3 inches in diameter make for simple lighting for the backside of the Track T. Wiring was easy as well with just three wires per light. One wire for brake lights and taillights, another wire for turn signals, and a ground wire.

5

Headlight wiring includes three wires (high-beam and low-beam) that originate from the fuse panel and through the dimmer switch and a ground wire. All three wires run through the headlight conduit and into the headlight bucket. Connections to the opposite side headlight are made inboard of the fiberglass nose.

6

Since the headlight buckets and their mounting brackets will need to be removed when it is time to paint the body, it makes sense to use a bullet-style connector (not shown) that can be disconnected inside of the headlight bucket to connect the headlight.

7

This inline fuel pump simply has two electrical connections to make: one power, one ground. It has since been replaced and a relay installed to keep from burning up the fuel pump.

8 Since no dash panel was included with the Track T kit, one was hammer-formed out of a piece of sheet metal. It was later replaced by a more refined version that was made of aluminum. The gauge design was first laid out on the dash, revised as desired, and then the holes were drilled out.

9 After the holes were drilled out, the gauges were checked for proper fit and then secured to the dash. For ease of serviceability, the dash panel was designed so that it can be removed easily.

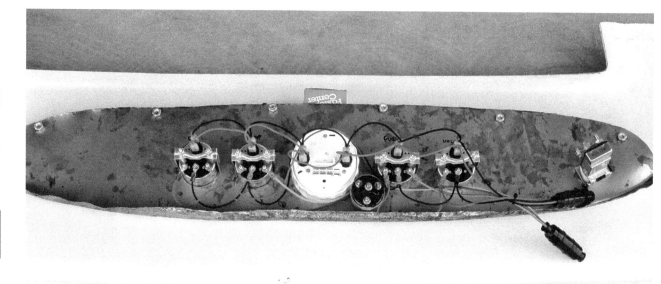

10 With the dash panel out of the vehicle, wiring the dash instruments and headlight switch was much easier and convenient. Quick disconnect plugs were used to allow for easy removal of the dash from the vehicle.

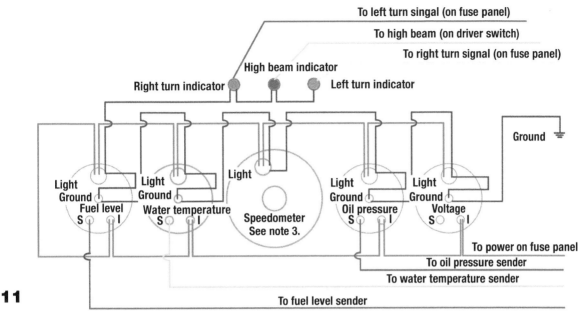

11

To left turn singal (on fuse panel)

To high beam (on driver switch)

To right turn signal (on fuse panel)

High beam indicator

Right turn indicator   Left turn indicator

Ground

Light   Light   Light   Light   Light
Ground   Ground   Ground   Ground
Fuel level   Water temperature   Oil pressure   Voltage
S   I   S   I   Speedometer   S   I   S   I
See note 3.

To power on fuse panel

To oil pressure sender

To water temperature sender

To fuel level sender

A color-coded schematic shows how the gauges are connected. Note that this view is as if you were looking at the backside of the dash, actually looking at the gauge connections. Also note that power from the fuse panel serves as the gauge sender for the voltmeter and can also be used to provide power to the rest of the electric gauges. Additional notes: 1."I" refers to "instrument power." 2."S" refers to "sender." 3. A mechanical speedometer will be cable driven and will connect at the back of the speedometer. An electric speedometer will have a combination of electrical connections that may differ among manufacturers. 4. Each electrical gauge will have a ground terminal that must be connected to a chassis ground. 5. The voltage gauge may or may not have a sender terminal as it receives its power from the fuse panel.

12

As we can tell from this photo, there is still lots of wire to be run and connected. All the more reason to use quick disconnects for the dash panel wiring so that the dash can be removed, especially in a smaller vehicle.

13

With the dash out of the way, it will be much easier to route wires through the body and beyond to their destinations.

14

Since there is *no* extra room under the hood, the battery was mounted in a marine-grade battery box and located behind the driver's seat back. Eventually, the positive battery cable will be routed beneath the floor and to a master disconnect switch located in the floor, just in front of the driver's seat. From there, the positive battery cable will continue to the starter solenoid.

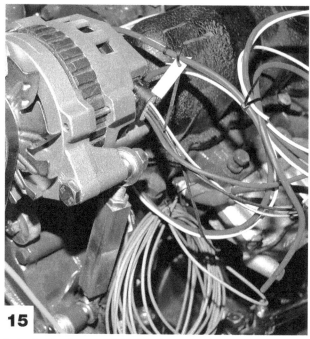

15

Red-and-white wires are routed to but not yet trimmed or connected to the alternator. Light blue and dark blue wires are for the front turn signals but not yet connected.

16

The two purple wires run from the fuse panel and connect to each of the terminals on the neutral safety switch that is integral to the shifter in this application. When adjusted correctly, the neutral safety switch prevents the vehicle from starting unless the transmission is in PARK or NEUTRAL.

17

A shifter boot covers the gap between the chrome ring and the shifter; however, more room was necessary to access the shifter and the neutral safety switch, so that opening was covered with an aluminum panel. Carpeting will eventually cover the aluminum panel. Located aft of the shifter is a floor-mounted dimmer switch that will be hand operated. Just beyond that, but out of the photo, is the horn button.

18

The fiberglass body of this Track T has reinforcing ribs to strengthen the floor. Since these are recessed from the top side, wiring was routed inside of them and secured in place with duct tape to prevent wiring "snakes" in the carpet.

19

Dual horns were installed with one on each side of the vehicle just beside the radiator. The metal mounting bracket served as a suitable ground. Although the horn power wire is not shown in this photo, it originates from the fuse panel and is connected to the horn button mounted in the transmission tunnel in the floor.

20

You know it is a small car when a little V-6 engine fills the engine compartment this much. The distributor is hidden beneath the plug wires behind the air filter, with the ignition coil and ballast resistor mounted to the firewall. Throttle and transmission kick-down cables were not yet connected. The mechanical fan was eventually replaced by an electric fan.

21

Although the engine is a German Ford V-6, the alternator is from a Chevrolet Cavalier. Like all alternators, power connects to the charge stud on the back of the alternator. An exciter wire and power wire connect via the plug in the side, with the two remaining wires not used.

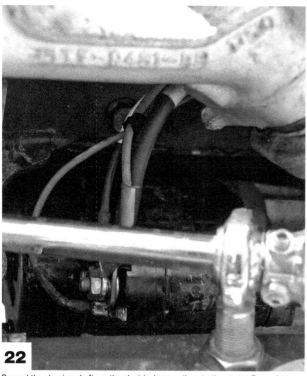

22

Beyond the steering shaft are the electrical connections to the starter. Power from the ignition switch and the positive battery cable connect to the main stud on the starter solenoid, while one of the wires from the neutral safety switch connects to a smaller connection.

23

Engine room is certainly at a premium in this vehicle. The distributor just clears the firewall and is surrounded by wires from the ballast resistor, the ignition coil, and the spark plug wires. When confines are this tight, you want to verify that your electrical connections are made correctly and securely the first time around.

24

With the hood sides removed, we can see that the engine compartment is full, top to bottom. All wiring is complete, including the electric fan and lights.

25

The negative battery cable actually connects to a bolt between the transmission and engine block that are not seen in this photo; however, the chassis is also grounded to a bolt on the front of the engine with a no. 4 battery cable.

All of the wires behind the dash have been cut to length, connected, and tied up out of sight. Foil-faced insulation covers any wires that run along the floor. Carpet was yet to be installed at this point.

26

A shot of the trunk area shows the fuel tank and various ground wires. The battery box is located between the passenger compartment and trunk area bulkhead and the seat back.

27

28

The finished version of my former '27 Ford Track T. The bulk of the buildup was documented in my book *How to Build a Cheap Hot Rod*, with the bodywork and painting documented in my most recent book, *Hot Rod Body and Chassis Builder's Guide*.

You may be working on a vehicle (street-driven or otherwise) that you would like to wire completely by yourself. If you are knowledgeable of the principles of electricity and have a clear understanding of how various components work, there is no reason why you could not design a complete wiring system for that vehicle. You would be well advised to sketch out all of the circuits in schematic form before doing any hard wiring. You can certainly visit your favorite electrical supply house and purchase an empty fuse panel to base your custom wiring harness around. Then add wiring, relays, fuses, capacitors, circuit breakers, and solenoids as necessary to perform all the tasks you desire.

ENGINE

Your custom-designed wiring harness may vary a little or a lot, but there are going to be specific areas to which you will be running wires. The engine compartment will typically include wires that go to the alternator, starter, and battery. On engines that do not have an HEI distributor, there will also be a 12-gauge wire to the coil. Depending on the type of alternator that you are using, the alternator will be the destination for two or three wires. For an alternator that uses an internal voltage regulator (commonly known as a GM alternator), a 10-gauge wire from the fuse panel will connect to the stud on the outside of the alternator. A 16-gauge wire comes from the fuse panel, passes through a diode, and then plugs into the alternator. A 12-gauge wire from that same plug also connects to the stud to which the 10-gauge power wire is connected. For externally regulated alternators, the wiring is the same, except that the 16-gauge wire from the fuse panel connects to terminal on the external voltage regulator. Another pair of wires then connects the voltage regulator to the alternator.

Wiring to the starter consists of the positive or "hot" wire from the battery, a 10-gauge wire that runs from the fuse panel, and a 12-gauge wire from the neutral safety switch. A second wire runs from the neutral safety switch to the ignition switch via the fuse panel. The neutral safety switch is activated by the shifter and when installed and adjusted correctly, allows the vehicle to start only when the vehicle is in PARK or NEUTRAL on vehicles equipped with an automatic transmission. A similar feature used on vehicles with a standard transmission is tied into the clutch pedal.

For a poor man's theft deterrent, a toggle switch can be installed easily in this wire between the neutral safety switch and the starter. If used, it should be installed where only the authorized driver knows where it is located. It should be easy to reach from the driver's seat, but not necessarily out in the open. A word of caution is that this security device should not be installed until after the vehicle has been thoroughly road-tested and all possible wiring problems diagnosed. At such time that the wiring has been proven to work correctly, the toggle switch is easy enough to install. You just have to remember to turn it to the ON position prior to attempting to start the vehicle, and then to turn it OFF when you park it.

There will also be wires to the temperature sender, the oil-pressure sender (for electric gauges), possibly an electric fan, and probably to a horn. A 12-gauge wire is common for providing power to the electric fan (if used) and also to the horn. Both the electric fan and the horn circuit need to have a relay installed. Sometimes these relays are included in the fuse panel, while sometimes they are not. A water-temperature sender can be threaded into a port in the cylinder head. A 16-gauge wire connects to it and runs to the temperature gauge or warning light. Oil pressure is captured by an oil-pressure sender that is threaded into a pressurized oil galley. Similar to temperature, a 16-gauge wire runs to the oil-pressure gauge. For mechanical gauges, the senders are similar (yet different), and then tubing connects to the gauges.

EXTERIOR LIGHTING

Wiring the headlights and taillights isn't difficult, but it does require a little more concentration, or you will find yourself making changes in your wiring just to connect the other light. A 12-gauge wire from the fuse panel supplies power to the headlight switch. Headlights and taillights receive power through the headlight switch. Courtesy lights (if used) are typically wired to be controlled by a door switch but can be wired to be controlled by the headlight switch as well.

From the headlight switch, a wire runs to the dimmer switch, which is usually mounted on the floor or on the steering column. From the dimmer switch, a 12-gauge wire runs to each of the high-beam terminals on the headlight pigtail. This can be done by running the wire directly to one of the headlights and then jumping over to the other light, or, if more convenient, running the high-beam wire to a point and then branching off in opposite directions toward each light. As long as your connections are secure, either method works just as well. In this high-beam circuit, a smaller wire will need to be run to connect to the high-beam indicator on the dash panel. For the low-beam headlights, another wire will originate at the dimmer switch and be routed to the headlights in similar fashion as the high-beam wires, but will connect to the low-beam terminal on the headlight pigtail. A ground wire to each headlight and to a suitable ground will complete the wiring of the headlights.

If parking lights are used, they each receive power from the headlight switch through a 16-gauge wire. If these lights are used as front turn signals, they receive their power from two separate terminals on the fuse panel. Either way, they must be grounded, whether the light socket is grounded through its mounting or if a ground wire is used.

Taillights are wired using the same basic methods as the headlights, but different connections are made. A 16-gauge wire runs from the headlight switch to each of the taillights. Just like the front turn signals, a 16-gauge wire runs from one terminal on the fuse panel to the left-rear turn-signal light, and another 16-gauge wire runs from another terminal on the fuse panel to the right-rear turn-signal light. The taillights and the signal lights may be combined in one housing or may be in separate housings. Each housing will need to be grounded, whether it is through the mounting of the light housing or with a separate ground wire. If the taillights and rear signal lights are in separate housings, misrouted wires should be the first place to check when diagnosing taillight or signal light problems.

Most late-model steering columns include an integrated turn-signal lever to which wires from the fuse panel are connected. If your steering column does not include turn signals, an aftermarket turn-signal mechanism that clamps onto the column could be used. This aftermarket accessory includes turn-signal indicator lights along with a hazard flasher and is wired just as if it were integral to the column. A push button for activating the horn can be placed on the dash or most anywhere that is within arm's length of the driver.

The brake lights are activated by a brake-light switch. Typically, the brake-light switch is connected electronically to the fuse panel, which automatically sends power to the brake-light portion of the taillight, through the taillight wire. It is conceivable that some lighting setups would require separate brake-light wiring. Since third brake lights are brake lights only, they require their own wiring, both power and ground. Although it is possible to include the third brake light in the taillight wiring, this light being illuminated when the running lights are on would defeat the purpose of the third brake light.

Brake-light switches used in hot rods are typically either a mechanical lever type or a pressure type. Both types are connected to the fuse panel by two wires, with the switch being open in normal operation or closed when the brakes are applied, thereby illuminating the brake

lights. The lever switch is installed after the brake pedal arm is installed and situated so that movement of the pedal arm pushes the lever on the switch. Space between the brake pedal arm and the lever dictates how long it takes before the brake light comes on. This may require some adjustment and fine tuning, but when it is adjusted, it can be forgotten. A pressure switch is plumbed into a "T" fitting in the brake line, so it can be installed as the brake lines are run, whether the brake pedal arm is installed or not. The pressure switch does not require adjustment; however, they are prone to failure and give no indication of malfunctioning unless a relay is installed with them. You don't want to find out that your brake-light switch failed by having another vehicle in your trunk or rumble seat.

ACCESSORIES

Electrical accessories for hot rods seem to have no limits, as more new products are available every year. Some of these accessories are safety related, while others are creature comforts. A windshield wiper and horn are safety items that are good ideas, whether they are legally required in your state or not. Other electrical accessories are air conditioning, stereo, power seats, power doors, air ride suspensions, and other items that are too numerous to mention. These systems all contain a fair amount of wiring of their own and therefore usually contain specific wiring instructions.

Whenever wires pass through sheet metal, a rubber grommet should be installed to keep the wires from chafing on the edges of the sheet metal. Grommets should be used on fiberglass as well, though fiberglass will require thicker grommets in most instances.

If you use heat shrink tubing to protect the connection, be sure to slide it onto the wire prior to crimping on the terminal. Also, be sure that you do not overheat or burn the wire when shrinking the protective tubing. If you burn the wire, you have defeated the purpose of using the heat shrink tubing in the first place.

As more wires are run along a similar route, use wire ties placed about a foot apart to keep the wires together and neat, adding more wire ties as more wires are added to the bundle. When running wires that will be located beneath carpeting or other upholstery, try to keep the wire bundle size small and flat if possible, to prevent having "snakes" in the carpeting. Wires that run along the floor can be covered with duct tape to secure them in place. Wires (including stereo speaker wires) that run behind upholstered panels should be routed behind any structural supports or roof ribs to avoid interfering with the proper fit of the upholstered panel.

(continued on page 120)

A simple principle of electronics is that the electrical component must be grounded to operate properly. If an electrical component is not operating properly, a faulty or no ground is quite possibly the problem. The ground cable of the battery should be connected to something substantial, such as one of the bolts that secure the transmission to the engine. A braided stainless-steel ground cable should connect the engine to the chassis, with another cable connecting the body to the chassis or the engine.

If the dash or gauge insert is built so that it can be removed easily from the vehicle (this is easier in some cars than others), wiring the gauges can be made easy. By using quick disconnects (such as those used for trailer connections) you can wire the gauges while sitting in your living room recliner if you desire, and then reinstall the dash when you are finished.

GAUGES

For electrical gauges, there will be three basic types of wires: those that connect the senders to the gauges, a power wire, and a ground wire.

Although there are many additional gauges available, the typical (and plenty sufficient for most vehicles) gauge package includes a speedometer, an oil-pressure gauge, a water-temperature gauge, a fuel-level gauge, and a voltmeter gauge. The speedometer is usually driven by a cable that runs from the transmission, and can be mechanical or electrical. For a mechanical speedometer, the cable contains a flexible shaft that is limited to broad, sweeping curves in its placement. Depending on the available room behind the speedometer, it may be necessary to obtain a 90 degree adaptor in order to keep from kinking the cable where it connects to the back of the speedometer. The cable for an electric speedometer contains a group of wires rather than a flexible shaft, which can make the cable easier to route.

Sender wires for the other gauges are typically a single 16-gauge wire that runs from the sender to the gauge. The oil-pressure sender is located on the engine block, and is threaded into an oil galley. A water-temperature sender will usually be located on one of the cylinder heads. The fuel-level sender is part of the float assembly. Note that the fuel-level sender typically has its own ground stud and therefore requires that a ground wire be connected to it. Turn signal indicator lights receive their signal from the fuse panel, while the high-beam indicator receives its signal from the dimmer switch.

For the voltmeter, the sender is actually a wire from a specified terminal on the fuse panel and is connected to the gauge or instrument power terminal on the gauge, rather than a signal terminal. Electrical power is indeed the signal for the voltmeter, but all of the gauges need electric power in addition to their signal feed to operate. This electric source can be wired in series from the voltmeter to the oil-pressure gauge, the speedometer, the water-temperature gauge, and the fuel-level gauge, as well as others. It can also be continued to serve as power for the dash lights.

Like all other electrically operated items, the gauges and their lights need a ground to operate correctly. Just like the power wire, but connected to the ground terminal instead, the ground wire can be run in series from one gauge to the next. Since the gauges are our monitoring system and therefore are our warning if trouble is brewing, we should take extra care to ensure that the gauges are grounded properly. If they are not properly grounded, we might mistake their faulty operation for a more serious problem that doesn't really exist. Of course, we should not assume that an abnormal reading of a gauge is actually a gauge problem either. In other words, make a mental note of what the typical readings are on your gauges, and then you will have a better idea of when something is wrong.

WIRING INSTALLATIONS

Chapter 9
How to Install Mobile Electronic Accessories

By Jason Syner

If you're anything like me, then Christmas and birthdays are all about getting the latest gadgets and toys that are coming out. If it's new and hot, then I want it and I want to know how I can use it in my car. This includes cell phones, game systems, navigation, computers, and iPods. I practically live in my car, so it's really important for me to be entertained and well connected while I am out driving around.

Most mobile electronic accessories can easily be installed with a cigarette lighter connection for quick plug-and-play. You can find affordable accessories to help you zip through traffic a little faster, or you can invest in high-end ones if you need your "James Bond" ego stroked a little bit. Let's take a look at some of the more common accessories you may want to use to complement your rocking sound system.

GPS

Quickly becoming a staple item in the average American driver's car is the GPS, or global positioning system. The more reliable, user-friendly, and consistent brands of GPS are TomTom and Garmin. GPS devices are supposed to help you find your way through traffic and give you directions to your destination—but remember, these devices rely on software updates. This means that periodically you must take them out of your car and hook them up to your computer so that they can keep current with changes to destinations, roads, and traffic patterns. If you don't update the software frequently, then chances are good it will eventually steer you the wrong way.

Some of the more advanced GPS devices give the ability to use a Bluetooth connection between your cellular

Here is an example of a common GPS unit, a TomTom, mounted to a windshield. These little navigational devices are great for finding your way around or even for locating specific businesses, such as gas stations and grocery stores.

phone and the GPS unit. When this Bluetooth connection is established, you can accept and place phone calls through the GPS device and have the audio broadcast through the GPS device's internal speakers. Some GPS devices have an audio OUT connection. This connection can be connected to a car's auxiliary IN connection, which is located on the dash of many new vehicles. Most GPS devices, including TomTom, will only let you transmit the cell phone call through the GPS' internal speaker. It will, however, allow you to transmit MP3 music and audio books stored on the GPS device through the car's audio system. Another way you can connect the GPS to the audio system is if your vehicle is newer and has an auxiliary (AUX) input on the dash. With this input, you'll need a mini, 1/8th-inch input plug. You'll then run the audio output from the GPS to this input on your dash. This is a relatively inexpensive cable, and you can purchase it at Radio Shack or Best Buy.

If this is a feature that appeals to you, then I recommend hard-wiring your GPS device to your car in order to help the audio streaming through the device operate more effectively. Most GPS units have a built-in modulator, or transmitter. This handy feature will broadcast your Bluetooth music (MP3s) through your audio system. You can do this by turning your FM dial to one of the lower stations (between 85 and 90 on FM) to pick up the audio stream on a dedicated frequency.

BLUETOOTH

You don't have to have a GPS device to install a Bluetooth connection in your car. There are other accessories available to help you talk and listen on your cell phone through your car's audio system. Bluetooth devices usually come as a plug-and-play kit that attaches to either your dash or sun visor. Motorola makes a decent kit, which can be bought for under $120. I do recommend making sure that your cellular device will work with your Bluetooth device before purchasing a kit. Many cellular stores can assist you with choosing the right in-car Bluetooth kit to work with your phone.

Your other Bluetooth option is the professional-grade hands-free kit called Parrot. Parrot makes several different models that range in price from $100 to $500. These kits enable you to play MP3 files, as well as send and receive cell phone calls through your audio system in your car while driving. Another cool feature of the Parrot kits is that they have a voice recognition system that you can use to dial contacts. When you accept any Bluetooth call through a Parrot or GPS system, you will have a caller ID function as well. This can help you decide if you even want to take the call while you're driving.

The Parrot kits are designed to be installed professionally and are hard-wired into a car. They are not designed to be plug-and-play installation. You could compare the wiring of these to that of an alarm system. It can be a lot of work, so if you're not comfortable doing this kind of work, let a retailer do it for you.

It's pretty safe to say that these days most new high-end vehicles come with an OEM Bluetooth integration system comparable to or better than a Parrot system. Let's take a look at how to set up a Bluetooth connection between a cell phone and a GPS unit.

This is a TomTom Go 920 GPS unit and a T-Mobile BlackBerry Curve. You can connect these two devices via Bluetooth by following a few simple steps. Even if you don't own these particular models of GPS and mobile phones, the Bluetooth connection setup process will be roughly the same.

1

On the BlackBerry phone, start the connection process by going into the phone options menu and selecting Bluetooth settings.

2

Under the Bluetooth options, select "Add Device."

3

The BlackBerry will ask if you will allow another device to find it, and you should select "OK."

4

The BlackBerry will begin to search for available Bluetooth-enabled devices.

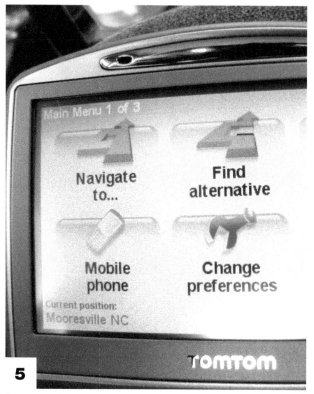

5

Next go to the TomTom's options menu and select "Mobile Phone."

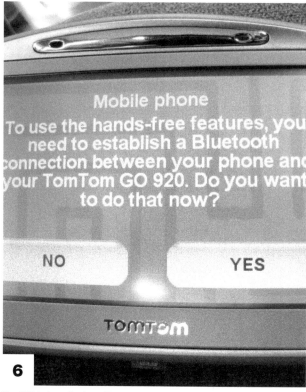

6

The GPS device will ask you if you want to establish a Bluetooth connection between it and your phone. Press "Yes."

7

The GPS will then ask if you want it to start searching for a phone, and you will also select "Yes."

8

The GPS will search for a mobile phone once you have given confirmation to do so.

9

The GPS and the BlackBerry will begin to search for Bluetooth devices in unison. If this doesn't happen, turn off the devices, reboot, and begin again. You have to work quickly if you want the devices to search simultaneously.

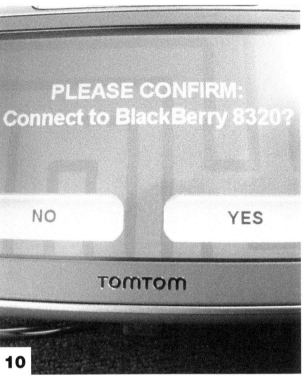

10

The GPS will ask for confirmation to connect to the BlackBerry smart phone. Select "Yes."

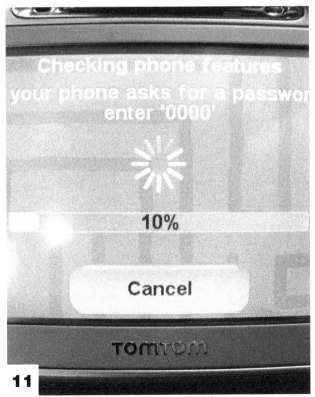

11

The GPS will begin a connection process to the BlackBerry, which should take a couple of minutes to complete.

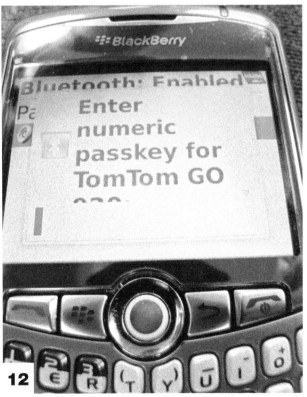

12

Often the device that you're connecting by Bluetooth will ask for a numeric passkey. The default numeric passkey for most devices is 0000.

13

The BlackBerry will ask you if you want to accept the connection from the TomTom. Click "Yes."

14

Once the devices are connected, you will see a confirmation screen showing that the devices are synched and ready for hands-free calling. In addition to being able to do hands-free calling and having access to the phone's address book by the GPS' on-screen menu, you will also be able to download weather alerts and real-time traffic information (provided your cell phone is equipped with a data plan).

15

Next the TomTom will ask you if you would like to copy your phonebook to the TomTom Go for easier hands-free dialing.

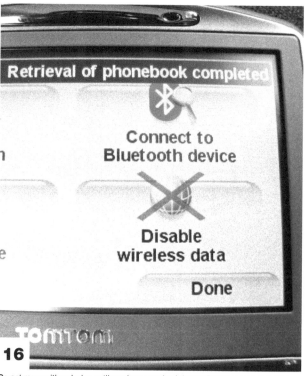

16

Do not move either device until you have received the confirmation message that the retrieval of the phonebook is complete.

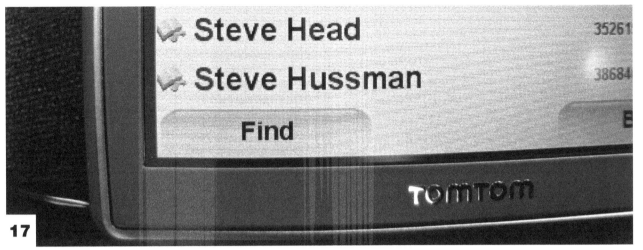

17

The full BlackBerry phonebook is viewable on the TomTom, and you will then have one-touch dialing. You can also talk to your contacts through the TomTom's internal speaker phone.

iPODS AND MP3 PLAYERS

Another popular device that has become a staple to most car audio systems is the iPod. These little MP3 players often hold your entire music collection—at least they do mine. I always hate when I get into a car that doesn't have an iPod connection, because that means you are at the mercy of looking for a CD or turning the radio dial. In this high-tech world, those are just not ideal options.

Many source units now come with iPod connection capability, although you do have to pay a little more for that feature. Likewise, you can buy a cigarette lighter adapter kit for any iPod (or any other MP3 device for that matter). The reason I like to connect my iPod directly to the source unit is that it eliminates a lot of the wires running across my dash. You can keep your driving space tidy while still using your iPod library. Pioneer makes an affordable yet quality source unit with an iPod connection (the DEH-P510UB), and it's really easy to use.

ALARM SYSTEMS

Before you go and add too many accessories to your car, I highly recommend adding an alarm system. Unfortunately, in the world we live in, you can never be too careful. If you are going to invest in a quality sound system and cool accessories, then you need to protect your investment. A decent alarm system can be bought for around $100 plus the cost of installation. Some retailers will install your alarm for free with the purchase of the alarm, or vice versa. The great thing about an alarm system is that it can give you power locks and remote keyless entry—even if you don't already have those features in your car. Clifford is the best alarm device money can buy, but Viper is a great choice because it provides supertight security at an affordable price.

You can purchase source units that allow you to connect your iPod directly to them. The owner connected this iPod to an aftermarket source unit. In many vehicles, this same connection may be located somewhere else on the dash; it is not always going to be found at the source unit.

Radar detectors are usually mounted on top of the dash, near the steering wheel, or, as shown here, they can be molded into a custom fiberglass gauge-pod. *Joe Greeves*

Radar Detectors

Much like car alarms, radar detectors have been around for a while, and the technology just keeps getting better. Beltronics makes an awesome radar detector that delivers long-range protection on all radar bands, including X, K, KA, KU, and POP. Just keep in mind that a radar detector is not your free card out of a ticket. It is not an excuse to speed or drive like a maniac, and the police can still catch you. However, if you like the added security of knowing who is around you, then I recommend the Beltronics RX75 Remote. Just be sure to check that detectors are legal where you drive.

ACCESSORY ADAPTERS, POWER SUPPLIES, AND WIRING

You may be thinking that all of these accessories are going to clutter up your car. Well, you're correct. There are few ways to deal with the mess of wires. Most cars only have one or two power adapter plugs, and if there is more than one, they are usually not located next to each other. This means that if you need to utilize both of them you will have wires running to two different places. Instead of having your wires running all over the place, you can buy a multiplug adapter for your cigarette lighter connection and then zip tie the wires up in a nice, neat line.

The multiplug adapter for a cigarette lighter power supply converts one power supply into two adapters, so you can use more than one accessory at a time. These are pretty inexpensive and can be found at Radio Shack.

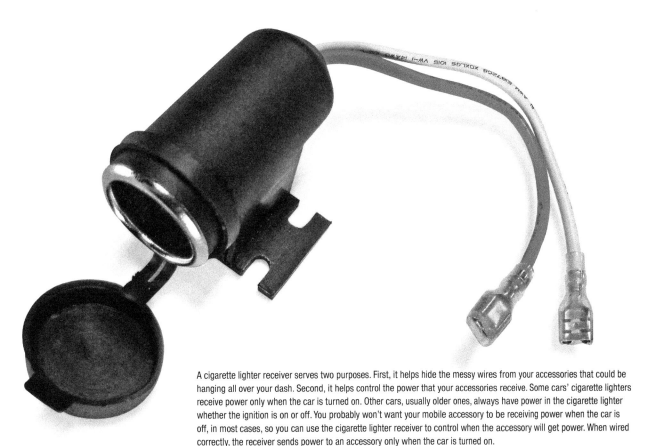

A cigarette lighter receiver serves two purposes. First, it helps hide the messy wires from your accessories that could be hanging all over your dash. Second, it helps control the power that your accessories receive. Some cars' cigarette lighters receive power only when the car is turned on. Other cars, usually older ones, always have power in the cigarette lighter whether the ignition is on or off. You probably won't want your mobile accessory to be receiving power when the car is off, in most cases, so you can use the cigarette lighter receiver to control when the accessory will get power. When wired correctly, the receiver sends power to an accessory only when the car is turned on.

These adapters can convert one power adapter to two or three adapters, depending on which one you buy. You can find these adapters at any electronics retailer. However, if you really want to make the dash look sleek and clear of the bird's nest, then I suggest hardwiring the mobile accessories directly to the car.

Typical Cigarette Lighter / 12-Volt Power Adapter Wiring

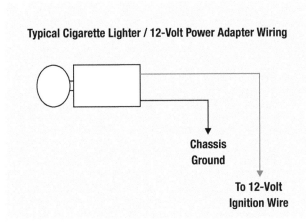

Chassis
Ground

To 12-Volt
Ignition Wire

This diagram illustrates how to hardwire an additional power adapter plug to your vehicle. Doing this will enable you to plug in devices that will turn on when you turn your key on and turn off when you turn off the key. The red wire is the power wire for the adapter and should be wired to the car's ignition wire that has 12 volts present on it with the key on and no voltage present with the key off.

All accessories plug into the cigarette lighter adapter, which provides 12 volts of power to the device. The plug that goes into the cigarette lighter connection has two prongs on the end. These prongs are ground connections. The center pin on the end of the plug is your 12-volt power. Most auto parts stores have a cigarette lighter receiver connection that is a female plug and you can plug your cigarette lighter cord into. This plug has positive and negative wiring that comes off of it. You'll want to take the negative connection and connect it to a chassis ground point (bolt) and tighten it down.

Note: The color and location of the 12-volt ignition wire can be found by consulting the service manual for your vehicle. Service manuals are available at dealers and most auto parts stores.

Then connect the 12-volt wire to one of the switched ignition wires coming off the steering column that will have 12 volts of power when the key is on. (When the key is off, the wire will have zero volts of power.) While at the auto parts store, be sure to purchase a low-amp fuse (around 5 amps) so that you can wire it in-line on the positive lead. Once the two wires are connected, tuck them behind the dash and feed up the power plug for your device and plug it in. Once you've completed these steps, you'll be able to turn on your car and have your GPS device automatically start up and be ready to go.

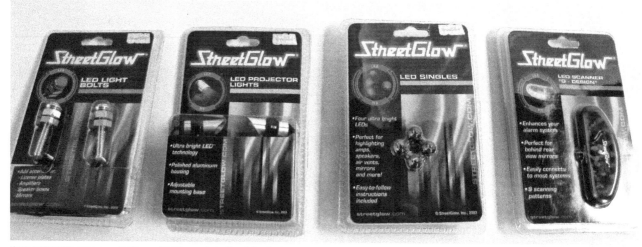

Here are four different types of LED accent lighting made by StreetGlow that you can purchase for your car. Left to right, the first is an LED light bolt, which is a bolt with a nut that you can use to secure an amp or speaker to your vehicle. The center of the bolt lights up with the color LED of your choice. The second item is an LED projector light that has an adjustable base that allows you to point the glow of the lighting to shine wherever you would like it to. The third items are LED singles, which are four individually housed LED lights that are tiny enough to place in very small places and still get a very bright accent glow. The last item is an LED scanner, which is small plastic housing filled with LED lights. These lights have nine different patterns and pulses, which flash to create different effects within your car.

A little accent lighting can go a long way toward drawing attention to your system. This picture shows EL (electroluminescent) lighting that has power lighting it up in the hatch of a Civic. This lighting really stands out in dark spaces.

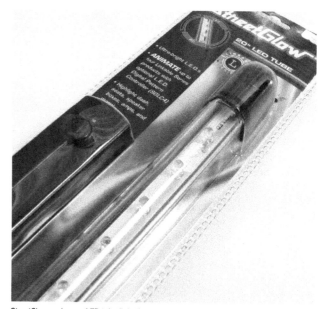

StreetGlow makes an LED tube light that mounts to the vehicle's undercarriage for exterior accent lighting. This is similar to neon but has a brighter glow. It looks really cool at night when you're driving down the road. However, you have to be careful not to use colors that will make you look like an emergency vehicle, such as blue, white, or red. Check with your state to see what neon colors are legal for the exterior of your car.

ACCENT LIGHTING

Accent lighting is a great way to show off the little details in your system and to bring a unified style to your interior's design. I often try to give all my components one, two, or three colors specifically. This way I can unite all of the components of my system in an artistic way.

Accent lighting can be as simple as getting all of the displays on your source units, gauge clusters, and dash computers to glow in the same color—or it can be as complex as adding LED lights behind interior trim pieces.

Radio Shack is a great place to buy LED lighting. You may also think about using electro-luminescence (EL)

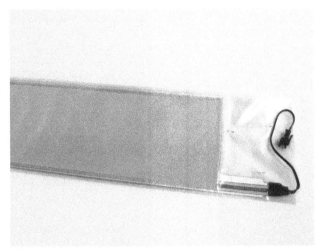

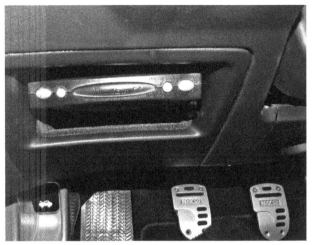

EL lighting that is not connected to a power source comes in a sheet, such as this one made by Razor Lite. The sheets can be cut with scissors into whatever shape you desire. This is really great to place behind cut-outs, especially if you want to place it behind the cut-out of a name or logo.

Neons and LED lighting can be controlled by remotes. This controller is made by StreetGlow and is made for neon/LED control. It enables you to change the color of the lighting installed on your undercarriage, as well as control the light to make different patterns for special effect.

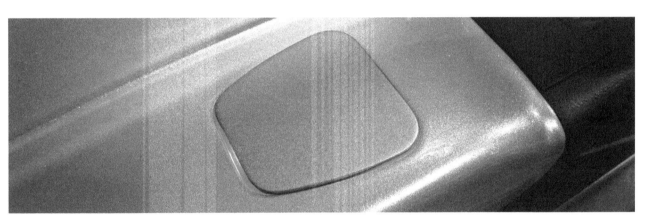

LED lighting is also a great highlight on the interior of a car, such as seen on this door panel. At night, this lighting can highlight the custom work in a car.

lighting. This type of lighting is more expensive, but it offers the most consistent light with the most reliability and flexibility for installation. Razor Lite (www.razor-lite.com) is a great source for EL lighting.

Neons are another popular choice for accent lighting. StreetGlow is a great manufacturer for neons because their products last a really long time and are very affordable. You can purchase StreetGlow products at Advanced Auto Parts stores. The company makes neon products that can mount to your undercarriage in the form of tube lights, and they also make interior accents lights.

COMPUTERS AND THE INTERNET

Another cool new wave of technology growing in popularity with mobile electronics enthusiasts is integration of laptops and other computing devices into car systems. Adding a laptop to a car can be important, due to the amount of next-generation communication tools that are available with the Internet, such as Web TV, Web search, e-mail, and social networking. Also, you can now control your home's security system and other electronics by Internet connections when you use special software.

So imagine if on your way home from work while you're sitting in traffic, you are able to log into the IP address of your stove and begin preheating your oven for dinner. You could even pull up in front of your house and disarm your home security system from your car, while still being able to monitor high-priority work e-mails.

Most cellular phone companies offer wireless Internet cards that are USB 2.0 compatible, which gives you mobile Internet access even when you're in your car. You can also buy a DC-to-AC power converter so that you can plug your laptop into your car and avoid having to run off of its battery.

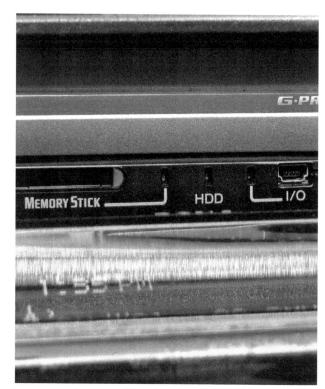

On the Sony MEX1HD, just hit the open button on the face to access the data ports behind the face, as shown in this picture.

As you can see, the memory stick slot is on the left, and the USB 2.0 connection is on the right.

If you want to take car PC technology to a higher level, you can even build a PC into your car's dash. To do this, you'll need to buy a computer case and then find a place to install it in your car that will not have too many vibrations (as this can damage the motherboard). You will also need a power supply designed to run off of 12V DC, a motherboard and video card with composite video output, a video screen, a hard drive, and a touch mouse. The audio for the PC can be integrated into the car's stereo system. To help you shop for these parts, try visiting www.mp3car.com. The hard drives sold on this website are designed to protect against moisture, humidity, voltage and power surges, and temperature changes. I highly recommend buying PC components from them, as they are designed to be inside a car.

It is important to remember that using a laptop while driving can be very distracting for the driver, so if you decide to incorporate this type of technology into your car, be sure to comply with all recommended safety standards.

Some car stereo manufacturers create source units that accept a wide variety of media formats. These source units make it possible for you to play more than just music from them, but also access digital photos, movies, MP3 files, or any other kind of media files. Usually these source units also have a display screen so that you can view these files. Sony makes a model called a MEX1HD that has an integrated memory stick port and a USB connection. This allows you to import MP3 files directly to the unit's internal hard disk from a memory stick. By making your digital media files mobile, you can be sure to have them on hand anywhere you go.

REMOTE KEYLESS ENTRY

Mobile electronics can include many different types of accessories with various functionalities. For example, a really cool accessory is remote keyless entry. If you have a car that didn't come standard with this feature, then you know what I am talking about. Having to manually lock and unlock your car is a pain in the neck. But for as little as $135, you can add remote keyless entry. To do this, you must buy a $35 door-lock actuator to control the manual-lock function in the car doors. Then you wire a $100 remote keyless entry kit to the actuator to make the locks work by remote control. If you do the labor yourself, you can really get this project done for a small cost. I suggest buying the Spal all-in-one kit that provides both the remote's keyless kit and the actuator. You should plan for this project to take about a day to get done.

Now if you already have power locks in your car but you don't have remote control keyless entry, then Micro makes a great remote keyless entry kit for about $60. This project should take you only around two hours.

On this Sony XAV-A1 source unit, the yellow 1/8-inch minijack can be used for any external audio and video source to display on the 7-inch touch screen, such as a video camera, laptop, iPod with video, or digital camera.

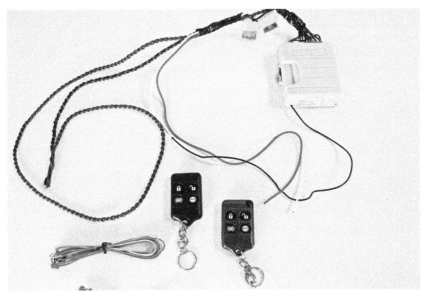

This is a Micro keyless entry system with two remote controls. It should be wired to the power and ground wires at the car's ignition so that it has constant power. The door trigger wires must wire into the factory power-door lock relays, to lock and unlock the doors.

This is a General Motors factory door lock actuator. If you want to get in and out of a vehicle by remote control, you can purchase a keyless entry system and wire it into this door actuator.

A back-up camera can be a great addition to a vehicle for added safety and driving visibility. To install a back-up camera, you should first have your video system installed in the car, connected, and powered. Connect the video cable from the back-up camera to your video LCD monitor. Next, move the camera around to the rear of the car until it shows the desired position on the screen. Once you have found your preferred position, you can mount the camera to the rear bumper of the car. Visor View makes many different back-up cameras, including ones that integrate into your license plate holder, making the camera less noticeable on your car.

Dakota Digital makes voltage gauges, such as the one in this picture. It has brushed aluminum and a blue LED display. They are really easy to wire, and they have only two wires, a positive and a negative. Just be sure to wire the positive wire on a switch so that you can turn the gauge on and off.

BACK-UP CAMERAS

A new security feature that many car manufacturers are promoting is the car back-up camera. This small camera installed on the back bumper of a car can act as a rear-view mirror but with much greater visibility. It also shows drivers their blind spots better.

You can add a back-up camera for less than $100, and they are outstanding if you already have a flip-out video screen in the dash of your car. You might look for a Visor View, which is a military-grade camera. They are easy to install and have great video resolution. You can get these installed in about two hours.

GAUGES

There are many types of gauges you can add to your car as an electronic accessory. There are the standard ones that read fuel pressure, air-fuel ratio, or water temperature, and other gauges that monitor engine performance. You can also add gauges that monitor your audio system's performance, such as a voltage gauge, a current gauge, or an amplifier temperature gauge. These gauges can be molded into any area of your car's dash, windshield, or center console. You can buy them so that the lighting matches the other interior lights in your car, or you can adjust your factory gauge lights to match your aftermarket gauges. I recommend gauges made by Dakota Digital because they are affordable, have the best-looking displays, and have many colors to choose from.

Mobile electronic accessories add the "wow" factor to a car. They are the devices that make people want to go for a ride in your car so they can covet the cool toys. And that's okay—if you work hard to create a cool playground, then by all means, play in it.

Don't forget that all of these mobile electronic accessories often come with remote controls to operate them. On the left is a picture of a Sony Joystick Commander, which belongs to a CDX-CD90 (Sony) source unit. To the right of that is a Sony handheld wireless remote control that controls a touch-screen source unit. The far right picture is a Sony Remote Commander, which comes with its own LED display and works with most Sony source units. This one is handy because you can control all the functions of a source unit from a remote location.

The toggle switches here were installed in a custom console on a black ABS plastic panel with LED indicator lights. These can be used to turn on amplifiers, lighting, or gauges.

MOUNTING A SATELLITE RADIO

Previously we discussed wiring your mobile electronic accessories in your car by utilizing the cigarette lighter connection or by hard-wiring them to your car. Once you have made a decision about how you're going to wire your accessory, you will need to decide where you're going to mount the device in your car. Let's walk through an installation of a Sirius satellite radio into a 2004 Honda Civic.

1

The first thing you need to do when you get a new accessory is unpack the box and check the parts list to ensure that all of your pieces are present and ready to go into the car.

2

Most electronic devices and accessories come with a "getting started" pamphlet. It's a good practice to read this document to familiarize yourself with the setup procedure.

3

This is a Sirius satellite radio display's mounting dock and bracket. The satellite radio plug-and-play kits usually have two mounting options. You can either use a dash suction cup or adhesive mount, or you can use an AC vent clip mount on modern cars like our Civic. In this case, I used the clip mount.

4

Four set-screws attach the mounting bracket to the radio dock. An all-in-one tool (such as a Leatherman Wave) is useful for the assembly of mobile electronic devices. A Leatherman is a quick-access tool that gives you basic tools at your fingertips at all times. Of course, you would use it as a complement to a larger collection of tools, but a Leatherman is something you should always keep in your pocket.

HOW TO INSTALL MOBILE ELECTRONIC ACCESSORIES

5

Once you have assembled the mounting bracket and the dock together, you need to test-fit it on the AC vent to make sure it will fit and stay stable when you're driving. You also need to check and be sure that you will still have access to all of your steering controls (such as your blinkers) and that your steering wheel or any other mechanism of the car will not be prohibited from functioning properly because of the device.

6

All Sirius satellite radio kits come with an externally mounted antenna. This antenna must be placed outside the vehicle away from the other antennas. It needs to have a minimum of 3 inches of metal around it in all directions. The antenna wire must be routed to the interior of the car and should be placed underneath the weather-strip material around the front or rear windshield on newer cars like our Civic. You have the option of mounting this in the front or rear of the car.

7

I placed the antenna in the center of the roof, as shown in this picture. Once it is placed where you want it, you can begin running the wire.

8

A flat, plastic putty knife should be used to gently lift the factory weatherstripping so you can tuck the antenna wire underneath.

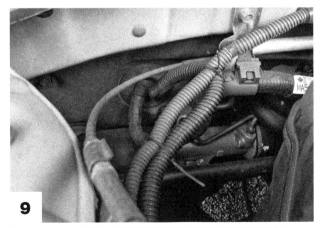

9

Now the cable is under the weather-strip material down to the bottom of the windshield and into the engine compartment in preparation for running it inside the car. At this point, you must search the firewall of the car and look for a thick rubber grommet (usually circular) where wires run through the center of it. This will be your point of entry into the interior of the car.

10

A long zip tie (around 3 feet) is a useful tool. Push the zip tie through the rubber grommet. Then go around to the interior of the car and look under the dash to see if you can see the zip tie pushed through. If so, then you know you have a clear entry into the interior. If not, then you need to find another grommet and try again. If there's a large bundle of wire going through a grommet into your interior, then 99 percent of the time it will be your best point of entry.

11

After confirming that your zip tie pushed to the interior, use electrical tape to attach the antenna wire to the zip tie, and then stick it through the hole in the grommet.

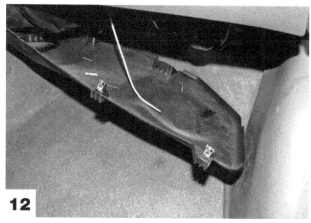

12

Remove the plastic panel underneath the dash to access the zip tie and the antenna wire and then pull it into the interior of the car.

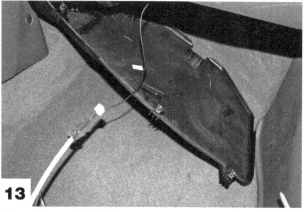

13

Make sure that you pull the zip tie and antenna cable gently and completely into the interior of the car. Also ensure that you connect the antenna wire and the power plug to the device's dock. Use zip ties to help tie up and hide the antenna wire under the dash so the wire is safely out of the way.

14

The power requirement for this electronic device is a standard cigarette plug, as shown in this picture.

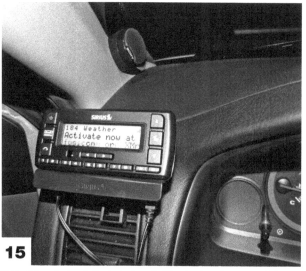

15

Connect the radio face to the dock when all of the wires have been connected.

16

As a secondary option, you can mount the radio to the center console, making it ergonomically easier to reach from both the driver and passenger seats.

LIGHTING

Lighting is a great way to draw attention to your car, especially if you add it to the exterior of your car. LED lights are very bright, so if you have them on while you drive at night you can be seen as a bright blur from very far distances. Let's take a look at how to add this type of lighting to a car.

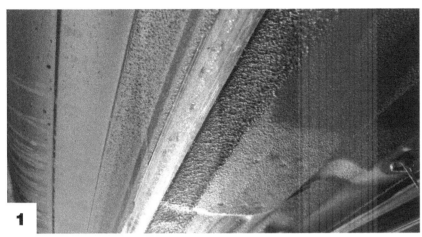

This is a 48-inch LED tube that is being placed underneath a car on the edge of the frame rail. This placement protects the tube, in case something flies under the car. If that happens, the rail gets hit instead of the tube. You will need to wire the lights to the neon controller that connects to the battery (see Chapter 2). Each lighting kit wires differently, so be sure to check the instructions that come with the kit to make sure you do it correctly. Usually, there is one wire that goes into the tube and one that comes out from the tube, and all wires are in series together. In this scenario, the power would come from the car's battery into the controller, out from the controller to the first tube, and then over to the second tube.

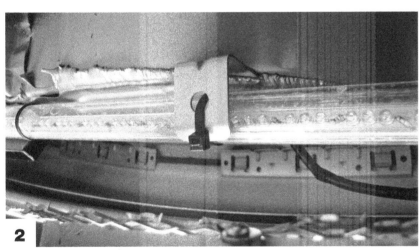

Whenever possible, use factory mounting tabs or brackets to secure the LED tube to the car. This will keep the tube from moving around while you drive.

Once you have secured the tubes to your vehicle, power the tubes and rotate them until you have the desired lighting effect.

This is a completed LED tube undercarriage installation with the power on, to demonstrate the glow.

Typical Neon Lighting Placement

Neon Tube Placement
Underneath Car

This chart shows the most optimal placement point for neon/LED tubes underneath a car. I always place the shorter tubes horizontally across the car left to right, and I run the longer tubes vertically front to back. I also try to mount them far enough under the car so that you can't see the tube; you can only see the glow from the light.

Mobile electronic installation can be a lot of fun for the enthusiast, but it is not without its fair share of headaches. You can save yourself a lot of time and grief if you follow this simple but highly important list of do's and don'ts. — Jason Syner

DO

1. Always place a fuse in-line on the power cable(s) between the battery and the piece of equipment you are connecting it to. If you don't, any metal that touches the end of the power cable that isn't fused will arc weld and leave you in a smoldering pile of dust.

2. Always individually place a fuse in-line between your fuse block and all connected pieces of equipment. This will prevent the equipment from shorting out.

3. Always bolt subwoofer enclosures and equipment racks to the car using grade-8 bolts. This will prevent them from shifting during travel or injuring you during an auto accident.

4. Always place weather-strip material on the mounting flange of speakers before installing them in their mounting location. This prevents air leaks and distortion of the sound and will increase the speaker's power handling.

5. Always use a heat gun and a roller when applying Dynamat. Heat the Dynamat with the heat gun and roll it completely flat. This will improve the performance of your sound-damping product.

6. Always run your power wires on one side of the car and your speaker wires and RCA cables on the opposite side of the car (from the power wires). This prevents noise from getting into the signal cables.

7. Always disconnect the battery before disassembling the car or doing any type of installation. This will prevent fires, deployment of the factory air bag, and malfunctioning of any other factory parts.

8. Always connect all electronic pieces to a good chassis ground point. This needs to be a structural piece of the car, such as the frame or seatbelt bolt, and the electronic pieces all need to connect to the same ground point. Make sure that you sand off all the paint from that point with a wire wheel and a drill. This is important because it prevents ground loops from occurring in your system and also prevents noise.

9. Always run a chassis ground when connecting a head unit to an aftermarket wiring harness. Do not use the ground wire at the aftermarket harness. If you're using an amplifier in your system, run the ground wire from the head unit to the amplifier's ground wire. This will prevent alternator whine from coming into your system.

DON'T

1. Never use any power tools without instruction and careful practice. This includes but is not limited to: hand tools, drills, routers, table saws, jigsaws, welders, grinders, and air tools. Always wear safety goggles—every day, all day while working on your car. Never take them off!

2. Never get underneath a car without multiple jack stands placed underneath the frame at the structural location. It's even smart to have a few backups in case you aren't sure of the weight capacity of your stands. Never, ever, *ever* use the car jack to support the car and then slide underneath.

3. Never have different sizes or types of batteries inside your car. If you have a starting battery up front and add a deep-cycle battery to your trunk, then they must have a battery isolator. If they are paralleled, then they must be the same type of battery with the same amperage.

4. Never mount a subwoofer with a drill and a screw. Always predrill the subwoofer mounting holes in the subwoofer box with a tiny drill bit. Then when mounting the subwoofer in the box, hand-tighten the screws with a screwdriver while cupping the screw with your opposite hand to prevent the screwdriver from popping off of the screw and damaging the subwoofer surround.

5. Don't ever drill through the floor of your car without getting underneath and checking to see what is underneath that area of the car. Don't drill in the vicinity of the gas tank or fuel lines.

6. Never run a power wire through an opening in metal without plastic conduit or a rubber grommet surrounding the wire as it passes metal. This will prevent a short in the wire or a car fire.

7. Never install neon lighting without fusing the power wire going to the neon tubes. A lot of neon tubes are extremely high voltage after the power transformer, so they must be used with caution. It is also a good idea to check with your local authorities to see which neon colors are permissible and will not conflict with emergency vehicles.

Appendix

TROUBLESHOOTING TIPS

Problem	Probable Cause	Solution
The points-type ignition won't start.	Points are fouled or out of adjustment.	Replace or adjust points.
There is a switch failure in high-current items such as fan, fuel pump, headlights, and horn.	Accessories are drawing more current than the switch can handle.	Rewire the accessories using a relay.
Fuses keep blowing.	The circuit cannot handle the overall load needed for all of the accessories.	Use relays to minimize the current within the circuit or run some of the accessories on a separate circuit.
A light bulb won't illuminate.	Faulty bulb.	Check a bulb with a multimeter or by trying it in another circuit. Replace if defective.
	Faulty connection between bulb and bulb socket.	Clean contacts on the bulb and socket.
The oil-pressure gauge reads full pressure, even if the engine is not running.	Faulty oil-pressure sender.	Replace the oil-pressure sender.
Power seats do not work.	Obstruction beneath seat preventing movement.	Remove obstruction.
	Blown fuse.	Replace fuse. If fuse blows again, check for other problems within the circuit.
	Faulty power-seat motor or switch.	Turn ignition switch ON, but do not start engine. Operate the power-seat switch and listen for motor noise. If there is no motor noise, check the switch. If there is motor noise, inspect the drive-assembly transmission, gears, and tracks. Repair or replace as required.
Key will not turn in the ignition switch.	Faulty ignition lock cylinder.	Replace ignition lock cylinder.
Warning lights on the instrument panel do not turn ON when the ignition key is turned to the ON position.	Faulty ignition switch.	Replace the ignition switch.
Intermittent cooling from the air-conditioning system.	Faulty low-pressure cutout switch.	Refrigerant level is probably low. Have A/C system recharged.
	Faulty compressor clutch.	Less than adequate battery voltage reaching compressor. Check wiring connections. Test for proper voltage with multimeter.
	Faulty compressor clutch relay.	Check wiring connections. Test for proper voltage with multimeter. Replace relay if it is faulty.
	Faulty A/C control switch.	Check electrical connections for good contact. If connections are good, replace A/C control switch.

Glossary of Terms

Amp: A measurement of current.

Basket: Frame and mounting flange of a subwoofer or speaker.

Channel separation: This is usually measured in decibels at 1 kilohertz (kHz). Any CD player between 95 and 100 dB is considered exceptional. Anything above 80 dB would be acceptable.

Current: Current flows on a wire or conductor. It is measured in amps.

Damping factor: This is the value that tells you how the amplifier controls the speaker. An average damping value is between 250 and 500. A more high-end damping value is between 800 and 1,000. An amplifier with a lower damping value will be affected more by the load of a loud speaker and can cause the amplifier output to change. The higher the damping value, the less affected the amplifier will be by the speaker load.

DC: Direct current.

Decibel (dB): A measurement of volume.

Farad: Measurement of the amount of storage inside a capacitor.

Frequency response: This describes the range of frequencies that the source unit is capable of playing. A safe, general requirement is 20 Hz to 20 kHz. This is the basic audible range of human hearing.

Hz: Hertz is a measure of sound frequency in time or the number of cycles per second. A frequency of 1 Hz is equal to 1 cycle per second.

Octave: The interval between musical pitches with half or double the frequency.

OEM: Original equipment manufacturer.

Ohm: Measurement of resistance a speaker gives an amp.

Ohm's Law: Defines the relationship between power, voltage, current, and resistance.

Passive crossover network: An electrical circuit that is made up of a coil, capacitor, and resistor.

Power: The rate of energy transmitted, the amount of current x voltage, measured in watts.

Resistance: Describes the amount of current that will flow through a component, expressed in ohms.

Signal-to-noise ratio: Compares music level to background noise level; the higher this ratio is, the better. The signal-to-noise ratio of a high-quality source unit would be 109. To explain this further, on this particular CD player, the noise present in the background would be one, or 0 dB, and the signal would be measured at 109.

Total harmonic distortion (THD): Should be less than 0.05 percent at full power rating; the lower the THD, the better the sound of your electronic component.

Voltage: What pushes current through a circuit.

Voltage preout: This describes the amount of voltage output on the RCA jacks. The higher the voltage, the better the sound quality and dynamic range of the system. The average would be 4 volts, with 8 volts as above average.

Watt: A measurement of power.

Waveform: The shape of a signal moving through a space.

Sources

Affordable Street Rods
1220 Van Buren, Great Bend, KS 67530
www.affordablestreetrods.com
620-792-2836
Wiring panels, wiring kits, various wiring components

High Ridge NAPA
2707 High Ridge Blvd., High Ridge, MO 63049
636-677-6400
Automotive parts

Karg's Hot Rod Service
6505 Walnut Valley Lane, High Ridge, MO 63049
www.kargshotrodservice.com
314-809-5840
Hot rod fabrication and construction

Morfab Customs
79 Hi-Line Drive, Union, MO 63084
www.morfabcustoms.com
636-584-8383
Hot rod fabrication and construction

New Port Engineering
2760 Newport Road, Washington, MO 63090
www.newportwipers.com
636-239-1698
Electric wiper motors

Painless Performance
2501 Ludelle St., Fort Worth, TX 76105
www.painlessperformance.com
800-423-9696
Wiring panels, wiring kits, various wiring components

Summit Racing Equipment
P.O. Box 909, Akron, OH 44309-0909
www.summitracing.com
800-230-3030
Automotive parts

Waytek, Inc.
P.O. Box 690, Chanhassen, MN 55317-0690
www.waytekwire.com
800-328-2724
Electrical wiring supplies, terminals, connectors, and accessories

Summary

The main purpose of this book was to remove the air of mystery that often surrounds electrical work for the automotive do-it-yourselfer. Having read this book I hope you now have the knowledge and confidence to perform everything from simple electrical modifications to completely rewiring your vehicle. As you dive into your first project, I hope you will find that not only are most wiring jobs relatively simple and easy to do, but they can also be quite enjoyable and bring the same feeling of satisfaction as any other do-it-yourself project.

Thank you again for buying a copy of the 10th automotive how-to book I have written for MBI. I hope you have enjoyed reading any or all of them as well as I have enjoyed writing them. If you have any questions pertaining to your wiring project, feel free to contact me at Dennis@hot-rod-garage.com and you may also check out my website at www.hot-rod-garage.com.

—Dennis W. Parks

About the Author

Automotive Wiring: A Practical Guide to Wiring Your Hot Rod or Custom Car is the tenth book from author Dennis W. Parks, who has been a freelance automotive photojournalist since 1985. His other books include How to Paint Your Car; How to Build a Hot Rod with Boyd Coddington; How to Restore and Customize Auto Upholstery and Interiors; How to Plate, Polish and Chrome; How to Build a Cheap Hot Rod; The Complete Guide to Auto Body Repair; and Hot Rod Body and Chassis Builder's Guide. Parks' writing and photography have appeared in numerous magazines, including Street Rodder, Hot Rod, Midwest Rod and Machine, Truckin', Rodder's Digest, Street Rod Action, Custom Rodder, Rod and Custom, Super Chevy, Custom Classic Trucks, American Rodder, and High Performance Pontiac. Parks is also the co-founder and editor-in-chief of Hot Rod Garage, LLC, which is an authoritative hot rod–related website at www.hot-rod-garage.com. He lives outside St. Louis, Missouri, and hopes to soon start construction of a 1955 Chevy pickup that he has had in storage for several years.

The author alongside his former 1927 Ford Track T roadster. Construction of the Track T was documented in *How to Build a Cheap Hot Rod* and *Hot Rod Body and Chassis Builder's Guide*.

APPENDIX

Index

Milton Keynes UK
Ingram Content Group UK Ltd.
UKHW051016241024
449911UK00002B/9